WHAT DO YOU DO DURING THE DAY?

WHAT DO YOU DO DURING THE DAY?

A Reminiscence About The Edinburgh
Gateway Theatre Company

MICHAEL ELDER

Eldon
PRODUCTIONS

Published in 2003 by Eldon Productions

ISBN 0-954-5568-01

Typeset in Allise and Berkeley
Printed and bound in Great Britain by
Mackays of Chatham, Kent

TO SHEILA
With admiration, gratitude and all my love

Contents

Acknowledgements

When you're writing something of this nature in these days of instant litigation, you have to ask yourself a series of questions concerning the people you're writing about.

(1) Is he/she dead?
(2) If so will his/her relations/dependants/partner(s) read this and if they do are they likely to sue?
(3) If (1) and (2) do not apply is he/she likely to sue directly for him/herself?

The only one I'm worried about is (3) so I've taken the precaution of providing copies of the typescript for those most likely to resort to litigation.

This doesn't apply to Sheila because the business of a wife suing a husband would probably raise legal problems which would cloud the issue here and no one would benefit from it except the lawyers, so to hell with that. All she has done is read the rough draft as it came off the word processor, sucked in a few breaths and said things like "You can't say that" or "I think you'd better tone this down a bit." And in each case I've obediently done it.

As for the others … Well, when I gave them their copies they immediately consulted with each other to ensure that none of them had the same lawyer and then went away satisfied that their target – me – was clear and vulnerable to attack from different directions. But their subsequent readings and comments have been invaluable, our discussions about the subject-matter sometimes sad, sometimes hilarious and always productive and I record here my intense gratitude to Pamela Bain, Tom Fleming, Norman Fraser and Marillyn Gray for their help and advice.

When I started this opus I was determined that it was going to be "warts and all". The fact that there are fewer warts now is due to them and the warts that are left are mine.

I think those last two paragraphs will eliminate any chance of litigation, don't you?

But talking about warts, none of these warts would have been exposed to the public gaze at all if it hadn't been for Queen Margaret University College Drama Department and their Head of Drama and Creative Industries, Maggie Kinloch, who now occupy the old Gateway Theatre, because they have generously part-funded the publication of these warts and I record here my gratitude to them for making it possible.

Introduction

Shortly after The Edinburgh Gateway Company closed there appeared a little orange book entitled *The Twelve Years of The Edinburgh Gateway Company 1953–1965*. This is an admirable publication. It isn't out of date because it's not the sort of book that goes out of date and it's a mine of information and anecdote. It contains details of how the Company was formed and run, written by four of the people most intimately concerned, a complete list of the plays presented and the artists taking part as well as many photographs of productions, but – and it's a big but – it has been out of print for years and since then there has been surprisingly little written about the Company. The so-called doyenne of Scottish theatre critics, Joyce MacMillan, in an article in *The Scotsman* on the history of Scottish theatre, failed even to mention The Edinburgh Gateway Company. One must assume that this was because references to it are sparse and not easy to find. Several latter day post-graduate students have done PhDs on the subject, but so far as I know none of these has achieved the public light of day. Yet The

Edinburgh Gateway Company holds a very important place in the history of Scottish theatre.

The sharp-eyed will have noted the date of the start of the Company from the title of the orange book. From there it's a short step to working out that 2003 is the fiftieth anniversary of its foundation. Some of us are planning a reunion as we did to celebrate the fortieth anniversary. We had a smashing time in the Gateway itself which was most generously lent to us for the occasion by Scottish Television and almost a hundred former members attended. I seem to remember getting to bed that night at about three a m. The fiftieth anniversary will also be held in the Gateway thanks to the generosity of Maggie Kinloch and the Queen Margaret University College Drama Department who occupy and maintain the building for the purpose to which it has become accustomed. We hope that the number attending the coming celebration won't be far short of the number for the fortieth which would show how good for your general health a spell at the Gateway was. The remarkable thing about the last party was not just the number who attended but the fact that so many of them held The Edinburgh Gateway Company in such affection and regard that they were prepared to come from long distances simply to attend a one-night bash.

But still, nothing in print for nearly forty years. Now, however, with that important anniversary looming, interest seems to be reawakening. Bill Findlay, a lecturer in the present Drama Department, has written a history of the Gateway Theatre itself and I thought I might indulge in an ego trip by writing a reminiscence of the Company. Between us we hope to fill a long-felt want.

So here it is. It isn't a well-researched, accurate history of those twelve years and it rambles a bit because memory's like that, roaming off into odd byways and coming back again when the spirit moves you. It's merely my own personal memories of that time which are very clear in my mind as they are in others' who worked in the same

12

place, so I apologise here and now if someone wants particularly to discover the date of a certain production, a complete cast list, a list of props and the lighting plot – though why anyone would want to do such a thing beats me. This book will be virtually useless for the purpose. Your only hope would be to go back to the original orange book which you can still pick up in second-hand bookshops if you're lucky. It's well worth it if you're at all interested in one of Scotland's most remarkable theatrical ventures, and since you're reading this I assume you must be. But I do hope my later reminiscence will help to revive happy memories for many, not only amongst the Company but amongst the audiences who came to see the productions so faithfully and enthusiastically during those twelve years.

My personal connection with The Edinburgh Gateway Company lasted for the first seven years plus one extra play, so further than that I am not competent to go. I'm not claiming to be competent even as far as I have gone, but here it is for what it's worth, and I just hope that some of those who shared those years with me aren't sitting reading this saying, "Silly old fool, he doesn't know what he's talking about. It wasn't like that at all."

It might be difficult to find a single person who could write about the latter part of the Company's life because there was a growing tendency in those later years for actors to be employed for a play rather than a season, so there are probably fewer people with a long-term love for the old place or who have a long-term view of what was going on.

I don't keep a diary, not one of the *Dear Diary* kind anyway, although I've always had an engagement diary and mercifully I've kept all those. It's surprising how bare facts written in them about opening dates, how long we rehearsed, what parts I played, what extra matinées we did, even how much I got paid (not much) have helped to stimulate my mind into other wider things. And I've still got my presscuttings books where I've tried to stick the good notices alongside the bad ones as a salutary reminder about the similar treatment of impostors. My photographs and programmes have all gone to the Scottish Theatre Archive at Glasgow University and seem to have disappeared from the ken of man.

I only want to say a couple of words – well, maybe a hundred or two – about the overall life and death of The Edinburgh Gateway Company. It wasn't a long life compared with the other Scottish repertory theatres which are still going strong and all started before it: the Byre in St Andrews (1933), Perth (1935), Dundee (1939), the Glasgow Citizens' (1943) and Pitlochry (1951). But The Edinburgh Gateway Company carried the banner for Scottish theatre alone during those twelve years. It produced more plays by Scottish playwrights (a quick check gives the number as 70, 23 of them premières) and employed more Scottish actors than all the other theatres in Scotland combined through the period. And it's important to remember that in the end it didn't fail. It closed its doors deliberately when the Edinburgh Corporation founded the Edinburgh Civic Trust, announced the formation of a Scottish theatre company at the Lyceum and appointed a member of the Gateway Company Council, Tom Fleming as its first director of productions. Then, and only then, did The Edinburgh Gateway Company declare its job complete. It had held the pass until something with more money – bigger but not necessarily better – could take over and it closed not with a whimper but a bang.

CHAPTER ONE

A Very Short Lesson in History and Geography

I can't remember how I got the job. I didn't audition for it. I'd have remembered that. I didn't have an interview. The more I think about it the more I come to the conclusion that *I must have been offered it*. If that's the case it's very conceited of me not to remember the offer being made and I apologise. Yet there are certain straws in the wind . . .

The Edinburgh Gateway Company was formed mainly by three people: Robert Kemp, Lennox Milne and Tom Fleming with James Gibson as producer. Now, there are four names to conjure with on a first page! I think two of them may have been directly involved in my fate.

James Gibson was a tradition in his own right in the Scottish theatre and there will be many "Gibbie" stories throughout this dissertation. He had worked with the Scottish National Players and in the West End as well as in America, playing John Brown to Helen Hayes's Queen Victoria, and had been mercifully unaffected by the latter two. I had first met him in 1948 when he came to the Byre Theatre in St Andrews to witness a performance of *Tobias And The*

Angel. I was seventeen years old and about to become a student at the Royal Academy of Dramatic Art. I was playing the Bandit which is one of those parts where you're no sooner on than you're off again and finished for the night. I remember meeting him in the Byre Theatre yard, an aspiring young actor overawed in the presence of this living legend of the Scottish theatre. He didn't give the impression of being a legend: small, gnome-like, dark hair barely touched with grey, spectacles and a cigarette dangling from the centre of his mouth, thoroughly unpretentious and ordinary.

I met him again at the Glasgow Citizens' Theatre in 1952-53 when we did the season together and we became close friends and rivals, racing each other to complete *The Daily Telegraph* crossword puzzle each day. The first play I did at the Citizens' was the première of James Bridie's last play *The Baikie Charivari*, swamped by star names such as George Cole, Ursula Jeans, Madeleine Christie, Andrew Keir and Roddy MacMillan. I was a little out of my depth in this august company. I played Toby Messan, the plumber's apprentice with approximately six lines. Gibbie played the Deil, most of it from the top of a very tall ladder behind a front cloth, peering through a full moon and apparently not at all worried by vertigo. He must have been well over 60 at the time. The part was full of incomprehensible Bridie lines which puzzled the audience and irritated the cast and vice versa, but which Gibbie sailed through with never a stumble. Racing on to the stage for the curtain call on the first night I knocked into a table on the set and sent flying an ashtray full of cigarette ends – people smoked a lot on the stage in those days: it gave you something to do with your hands. Gibbie arrived beside me, impressive in black gown and black helmet with horns and a weird Gibbie special make-up, all crossed coloured railway lines like Clapham Junction. He muttered disapprovingly as the curtain went up to subdued applause: "Messan, Messan, you're well named Messan."

Gibbie was appointed The Edinburgh Gateway Company's first director of productions. Actually there wasn't such a grandiloquent title in those days: he was merely producer. I have a feeling he was instrumental in getting me the job and he might well have been aided and abetted by Robert Kemp, the première of whose play *What the Stars Foretell* I'd been in at the Citizens' earlier in the year. Robert was Scotland's best-known and most prolific playwright in the 1950s. He was a lovely warm man with a mordant wit and a facile pen, especially when writing old Scots. Witness his famous adaptation of *The Thrie Estaits*.

There could have been another influence, though if so it would have been a minor one. Kenneth Miles had been appointed Company Manager of the new set up, having been Deputy Manager under Willie Mackintosh at the Citizens' and I knew him well. I'd lost a lot of money to him at poker in the Citizens' green room and maybe he felt he owed me something. But then again, maybe not. Kenneth always gave the impression of not owing anyone anything, least of all money. Poker is a game I'd never played before and haven't played since. I'm not totally daft.

That season at the Citizens' ended at the beginning of June with a performance of *Victoria Regina* for Coronation Year. I hoped I'd be asked back the following season. It wasn't that I'd been entirely happy at the Citizens', far from it, but after all it was Scotland's première repertory theatre and in those days the repertory theatres were about the only places you could hope to find any kind of regular work in Scotland. But from the end of that season the Citizens', which had been founded in 1943 by James Bridie primarily as a house for the presentation of all kinds of Scottish drama and which had continued to do so under the direction of Peter Potter, began to move away from its original remit. First under Michael Langham, who took over next season, and then later under successive producers it became more international and experimental and though I don't suppose the founders of The Edinburgh Gateway Company were initially aware of this change which was beginning to take place in Glasgow in the summer of 1953, it became more and more evident as time passed and it was therefore increasingly important that the Gateway Company should keep the Lion Rampant flying which had been its avowed intent from its first conception.

That summer I went back to the Byre Theatre where I'd started my career in 1944 – as a very young schoolboy, I hasten to add – to play in a new piece by A B Paterson called *The Herald's Not For Sale*, and I think it must have been during that run that I first heard via the jungle drums about the new rep company which was to be formed in Edinburgh.

Edinburgh was virtually unknown to me in those days. I'd been born in London (an unwise move but my parents, who both came from Dundee, happened to be there at the time) and escaped some of the Battle of Britain and all the later V1s and V2s by staying with relatives in St Andrews. But in the April of 1953 I'd married into Edinburgh, although Sheila always stoutly maintains that she's a Leither.

Certainly by the time the Festival came round that year it was common knowledge that Scotland's new repertory company was due to start at the beginning of October in the Church of Scotland's Gateway Theatre in Leith Walk. There were disturbed rumblings at this in districts like Morningside and much clicking of disapproving tongues. Dear, dear, what was the Kirk thinking about, giving over a place of frivolous repute to a group of irresponsible and disreputable play-actors? During the Festival I'd got a job on what was then a very meagre Fringe with the Christine Orr Players in the old YMCA Theatre in South St Andrew Street. You see how Edinburgh was beginning to get its hooks into me. Irresistibly and from all sides. The play was *Pearl for James* by Christine, a pleasant martinet who

18

chain-smoked and had a nicotine stain on her upper lip like a ginger moustache. She had worked for years as a BBC radio producer and she produced the play herself aided and abetted by her husband Robin Stark who had once played a Macbeth in the same theatre which drew one of the most vitriolic reviews ever written by Kenneth Tynan.

So far so good. But between hearing about the new Company and what happened next, I must have been made an offer I couldn't refuse and it's very strange that I can't remember it happening, where it came from, who made it, whether it was by word of mouth, telephone or letter, because the next memory-lighthouse gleams out during the three-week run of *Pearl for James* when I found myself summoned to a tea party at the Glover Turner-Robertson School of Speech and Drama in Eglinton Crescent, probably the most elegant part of Edinburgh's elegant West End. Now the Glover Turner-Robertson School – in many ways the forerunner of Queen Margaret University College's Drama Department – had been the only acting school in Scotland until the foundation of the Glasgow Drama College four years before. It was run by Annie Glover, very tall, very grey, very elegant like her crescent, very stately and not at all theatrical. She was the money behind the business – or her husband, a doctor, was – and she taught the students, almost all girls, how to talk and walk like young ladies. Aiding and abetting her was the redoubtable Anne Turner-Robertson, a short, stumpy, larger-than-life character who had won the second gold medal at the Royal Academy of Dramatic Art in 1911 and lost the chance of a brilliant theatrical career through a serious back injury. She was the partner who could stir the girls up, remove their inhibitions and sometimes drag performances out of them. I'd never met the two Annies, though my bride of four months, Sheila Donald, had been a valued student of theirs and was to become a valued member of The Edinburgh Gateway Company when she wasn't otherwise occupied producing children. The purpose of this sedate soirée was to bring together some of the members of the new Company, therefore I must have been regarded as a member of it at the time of the meeting, and it was in this staid Edinburgh drawing room with its high windows, expensive curtains and genteel furnishings – the house was Annie Glover's – that I first met Tom Fleming and Lennox Milne, both long associated with the Glover Turner-Robertson School. I remember Annie Glover introducing me to Tom and telling him that I was joining his new Company. "Ah, well, you're worth shaking hands with," said Tom genially and he did so while I thought, "I hope Annie Glover didn't hear him say that." Tom had had lessons from the Annies, had been in the navy during the war and then toured with Edith Evans to India before returning to his native Edinburgh. Tall, dark, well-built with the typical looks of a leading man and a magnificent voice, he tended to be changeable, at one moment withdrawn and monosyllabic, at other times the life and soul of the party, intensely funny and entertaining and the best speech maker I've ever heard for any occasion. I don't specifically remember being introduced to Lennox but I do remember the twinkle in her eye and the warmth of her personality. She was a former student of the Annies and had made a name for herself all over Scotland as a leading lady. She gave the impression of great height although she wasn't really very tall, just ramrod straight and surprisingly slight. She had a long, angular face which could seem hard and cold, enabling her to play witches, domineering matriarchs, madwomen and other assorted unpleasant characters which are so stimulating to portray but which were totally unlike her warm and generous personality and her rapier-sharp brain. I grew to love Lennox very dearly and respect her mightily as I think we all did.

We were making polite smalltalk and breaking lots of ice quite successfully in the gentle clatter of tea cups over which Annie Glover was presiding when TR (as she was always known but never to her face), not one to miss a dramatic effect, flung open the door and Entered (you have to give the word a capital letter) projecting loudly "God, give me sherry," a substance which till that moment had not been in evidence. From then on the scene was dominated by TR. I can't remember what she said, still less can I remember what we all replied, but I do know that by the end of that afternoon I had been told the date for the first rehearsal of The Edinburgh Gateway Company, that the play was to be James Bridie's *The Forrigan Reel*, that I was to play Walter Phillips and that the opening date was 7th October. I knew now that I was an official member of the new Company. What I didn't know was that that was me for the next seven years.

The Gateway. Beloved little theatre. And it was little in the context of its time. Not so little as the Byre Theatre with its 72 seats and maybe eight extra chairs in the gangway if business was brisk and the fire inspector on holiday. However, compared to the Howard and Wyndham number one touring theatres and even the number two variety theatres which I had worked in with the Fraser Neal Players on a Scottish tour in the summer of 1952 it was not a big theatre. But it existed, which most of the number two variety houses no longer did by this time. Most of them closed after the Fraser Neal Players had passed through. I don't think it was entirely our fault, though admittedly our standard wasn't mind-bogglingly high. There was already a dangerous adversary lurking in the wings: television. They were well named, those number two variety theatres. They came in enormous variety from the total grottiness of the Victory Theatre, Paisley where you had to walk on duckboards in the dressing rooms under the stage if the River Cart was in spate outside the walls, to the architectural gem of the delightful Opera House in Dunfermline, from the cramped Empire in Greenock to the vast echoing barn of the Palace in Dundee. Now, with the wonder of television becoming

21

ever more popular there was no place for the second-rate sort of entertainment these places generally provided and they closed in rapid succession. It was tragic for those who relied on them for a livelihood, the musicians, the comedians, the singers, the dancers, the chorus girls and boys, the backstage staff, the front of house staff and management, but it was inevitable, and perhaps trying to start a new theatre company at that particular time wasn't terribly sensible. But it worked, possibly because its smallness meant that the Gateway became the ideal size to run economically and effectively, although those responsible for its finances would probably never say it was easy.

The Gateway stood – or rather it still stands, now with a nice clean face and a new bib and tucker as the Drama Department of Queen Margaret University College – in Elm Row, a section of Leith Walk. Number 41 to be exact. If you were particularly myopic and/or absent-minded you could walk past it and never know it was there. There was a canopy, but not a big one with the single word Gateway built in to it. There were two pairs of entrance doors, flanked by what looked like ordinary shop windows which over the next twelve years were to exhibit photographs of actors and actresses, shots of the current production and our yellow-bordered playbills telling the non-myopic what was on. Let's go through that first set of doors. Immediately you lose most of the metallic clank of the trams clattering up and down the wide cobbles in the middle of Leith Walk. A stretch of marble floor leads to a second set of double glass doors which have above them four glass panels. On the leftmost of these is sand-blasted the word Roller and on the right is the word Skating which gives you a clue to part of the building's murky history.

It had started life as the New Veterinary College in 1888 until the venture failed and the students got absorbed into another place on the other side of town which had been established by a bloke called

Dick. By the time the College finally closed in 1910 Edinburgh was in the grip, as were most places, of motion pictures and the derelict New Veterinary College was taken over by an entrepreneur called Pringle who rebuilt the interior as a cinema and renamed it Pringle's Palace showing short silent films. It was at this time that the sand-blasting must have occurred because apparently Roller Skating, which was having as much of a vogue as the silent cinema, was introduced. Whether the customers roller-skated while watching the films is not clear, but as well as the skating rink there was a stage beyond the cinema screen so the roller-skating audience could also be entertained between films by variety turns. Three sources of entertainment for the price of one. Quite a bargain, though we don't know what the charges were. Over the next few years cinema, roller-skating, and variety came and went. At one point Mr Pringle must have roller-skated into the sunset, because the building changed its name once more, this time to the Broadway which seemed more respectable than Pringle's Palace and attempts were now being made to establish a cultural centre of the Drama, the latest move to make something reasonably genteel of the premises. It failed as thoroughly as had previous efforts of various kinds. The property was now owned by Andersons the stationery and packaging manufacturers who confined their own operations to the factory at the back and in 1946 the boss of the firm, A G Anderson, whether because he'd overextended himself financially or in an attempt to placate a troubled conscience, got rid of the entire property, except the factory at the back, by presenting it to the Church of Scotland. It's doubtful if this gift of what was rapidly establishing itself as a rather smutty white elephant was welcomed with loud cries of delight, but it was accepted and The Church of Scotland Home Board appointed a young minister, the Rev George Candlish, to run the place and, we presume, try to make it more respectable. Very soon George made one of the most significant appointments of the building's history:

the formidable Sadie Aitken, commissar of the Kirk Drama Federation, supporting pillar of and dreaded adjudicator for the Scottish Community Drama Association, became Theatre Manager and was to remain so for the rest of the theatre's life until it was sold in 1965 to Scottish Television. An example of Sadie's economical turn of mind was immediately evident. The Church's new baby was given another face lift and its name was changed from the Broadway to the Gateway. Questioned later as to why she chose the name, did it convey the idea of a new portal into a sunlit upland of culture and achievement, Sadie said no, it meant buying only three new letters, though she may have had reason to regret her decision because from then on she kept getting correspondence addressed to The Getaway Theatre.

For some years the Church tried to run the Gateway as a sort of semi-professional repertory theatre but by 1953 they found the burden, financial and probably moral, too much and had begun to look round for someone to take over the running of the theatre under a lease from the Church of Scotland which, apart from being the landlord, would have no responsibility for its conduct. That, in a nutshell, leads us to the early autumn of 1953.

Where were we? Oh, yes. Just passing under the Roller-Skating sign. Beyond these inner doors steps lead down into the spacious foyer. It's bright here and quiet. The metallic rattle of the trams has faded completely. Box office to the right, doors to the auditorium straight ahead, cloakroom to the left with beyond it a short flight of four or five steps leading up to an inconspicuous door in a corner which gives access to Sadie's office. Tread softly and reverently here because in the days when Sadie was not only Theatre Manager but also Company Manager to those many repertory companies, this was the holy of holies: Sadie's word was law throughout the building and she was held in respect and dread.

24

Even now, in 1953, with half her responsibilities shorn from her, Sadie is still vital to the success of the new Company. Over the years she has built up a huge network of Women's Rural Institute secretaries. Sadie has the biggest collection of Women's Rural Institute secretaries of anyone in Britain. If Sadie approves of a play the Company puts on, the secretaries get informed and bus parties are organised and the theatre is invariably filled. If Sadie disapproves then she keeps quiet and the bus parties stay at home and play whist instead. So Sadie is kept as sweet as possible, just to be on the safe side. She is still a force to be reckoned with. There is the story, possibly apocryphal, of the actor in one of the earlier repertory companies who, playing a butler, had to come on to the stage and say, "Mr Mucking Fedelman to see you, sir." On the first night, almost inevitably, he spoonerised it. He had hoped to be in the following play but when the cast list went up on the notice board his name wasn't on it. In fear and trembling he went to Sadie's office and confronted her.

"Miss Aitken, are you sacking me because I said fucking on the stage?"

Sadie fixed him with beady eyes, adjusted her spectacles to make them beadier and replied in her best Morningside accent, and Sadie's best Morningside accent was very good indeed.

"My dear boy," she said, "I'm not sacking you because you said fucking on the stage. I'm sacking you because you cannae fucking act."

To the right of that door is the entrance to the tea-room. Just a tea-room, though there is coffee and an assortment of soft drinks as well. Nothing stronger. This is still the Church's property. The tea-room is presided over by Mrs Tait, a very large lady with several chins, a hat and an expression of permanent disapproval. There are assorted middle-aged ladies who help Mrs Tait, and also her daughter Margaret who is smaller than her mother and doesn't have a hat or so many chins, but who is starry-eyed about actors. (These are the days when there is a difference. There are actors and there are also people called actresses and the difference will be followed unashamedly throughout our story even if politically incorrect. You know where you are that way.) Perhaps this is the cause of maternal disapproval. But there is another reason. Mrs Tait knows that there is a secret which threatens the success of her tea-room. Next door to the Gateway, through the tea-room wall, is the Windsor Buffet, owned by George Muir and his family, George junior and Mona and Max, and some time fairly soon after the opening of the Company, done so secretly that there is no record of the date or of who perpetrated the outrage, an additional wire was led from the legitimate warning bell from the prompt corner to the tea-room, through the wall into the Windsor so that those who had slipped out for a reviving draught at the interval could be warned to drink up and hurry back for the next part of the evening's entertainment. The Church's representatives of course knew absolutely nothing about this, although sometimes you could see them hurrying their guests through their drinks when the warning bell went in the Windsor. Co-operation at its best, and you couldn't have more co-operative and delightful neighbours than the Muirs.

We won't go through the wide doors at the back of the tea-room, partly because Mrs Tait wouldn't like us snooping around in her kitchen, and partly because we'll approach that area a little later in a flanking attack when Mrs Tait's busy pouring tea. We return instead to the foyer and approach the doors into the auditorium

And there it is. A wide space with a single block of seats raked downwards towards the stage with a gangway on either side. Down each side wall of the auditorium is a series of arches behind which seats used to be arranged to form boxes of a sort from which wealthier patrons could watch the films and the variety turns and avoid getting hit by roller-skaters. The auditorium undergoes several refits over the years. The arches are demolished, a central gangway appears, the seats become more comfortable and we get a new carpet. But that's later and not how it is when we start this morning. The double doors protrude into the auditorium and on either side of this entrance tunnel there is what is called the Shelf which is steeply raked upwards and has three further rows of tip-up seats. The Gateway holds an audience of approximately 500. The curtain is up at the moment so we can see to the bare back wall of the stage. Actually it isn't strictly accurate to say the curtain is "up". At this time it splits in the middle and goes from side to side. It'll be a season or two before we gain truly professional standards and have one that climbs into the flies. The proscenium opening is surprisingly wide, thirty feet in proper measurement, and an equally wide set of wooden steps leads up to it. In later years these steps are sometimes removed and replaced with an orchestra pit. The stage area itself is deep and has more than adequate wing space on either side. It's a good size: neither so big that you feel you need a bicycle to get from one side to the other nor so small that you're crushed together and, in one of Gibbie's many memorable phrases, so close that you get up each other's noses. There's a fly tower overhead which will fly as much scenery as we're ever likely to need. Still facing the back wall of the stage, the prompt corner is conventionally to the right with above it the electrician's platform and the lighting control system which is by no means new but more than adequate. It consists of four banks of five dimmer wheels each. Beyond the prompt corner, against the right hand wall of the wings an iron ladder leads up to this platform and then climbs higher to the fly rail. Upstage of the ladder is the dock door which leads out into a kind of indoor courtyard with huge double doors giving direct access to the lane at the back of the building. This lane runs down from Montgomery Street with the back wall of the theatre to the left. To the right is the back wall of the factory where Anderson's are still constructing stationery and cardboard boxes. There must be a front entrance to this factory somewhere because we never see anyone from Anderson's in the lane, not even a stationer or a boxer having a fly smoke. The pend runs through the row of tenement houses, and here every second Saturday night a lorry is carefully backed down the cobbled lane, with the scenery for each new production. It will later depart with the scenery finished with at the end of the run of the previous play. Montgomery Street Lane becomes a dead end just beyond the theatre building, but before you get there is the stage door, a small door with incredibly noisy panic bolts on its inside. It has to be handled very gently if you're trying to make a silent entry to the theatre in the middle of a show because it tends to rattle as noisily as a full size steel band but less musically.

Sorry. I didn't mean to leave you outside. Let's go back on to the stage. On either side in the back wall is a door leading out into the backstage corridor and we'll go through one of them now. Come through the OP one, the left hand one, or we'll get confused.

Straight ahead is a short corridor which leads to that noisy stage door, but before we get there we find a quieter door set in the left-hand wall which has a hatch in it. Every interval Mrs Tait or one of her assorted ladies or Margaret opens this hatch and offers the actors and actresses cups of tea or coffee. Business is usually brisk. Behind this door is the kitchen with a gas cooker the size of which would satisfy the Tattoo caterers at the Castle. Beyond the kitchen is the boiler house and a large number of spare rooms and halls, both upstairs and downstairs, in one of which we would later set up a full-size table-tennis table and play with a remarkable lack of proficiency. But at the moment everything beyond that door with the hatch is out of bounds to mere actors and actresses and we don't dare to cross the threshold. Mrs Tait is watching. We'll stay at the door which has led us off the stage and turn right.

Here's the backstage corridor with the downstairs dressing rooms leading off it to the left. Number one dressing room has now become the Company Manager's office. It's full of typewriters and filing cabinets – well, one typewriter and the filing cabinets are practically empty at the moment – and new blue-headed notepaper which says *Edinburgh Gateway Company* and it no longer looks as if it's ever seen a stick of grease paint in its life. To the left of the door into the Company Manager's office is the notice board where cast lists go up every fortnight, dressing room lists for forthcoming productions and there are instructions about what to do in case of fire. To the right of the door is a recessed area which contains the iron spiral staircase, painted red for danger, leading to the upper floor of dressing rooms which is a death trap if you're wearing a sword and late for an entrance. That spiral staircase will grab a sword and twist it between your legs as quickly as a pirhana grabs flesh. The girls generally use dressing rooms two and three on the ground floor beyond this spiral staircase, because it might be a little undignified for them descending from upstairs by such gymnastic means, especially if they're wearing crinolines. Dressing room three is the big one. It's big enough to hold four girls in comparative comfort, and somehow as the years go by it's this dressing room which becomes our sort of unofficial green room where we drop in during the show while waiting for an entrance. It's the one nearest the prompt side of the stage. The girls are invariably welcoming and hospitable, though there must be times when they're sick of the sight of us.

Up the spiral staircase are four other dressing rooms. Number four, to the right at the top of the staircase and above the Company Manager's office, is now the wardrobe, presided over by a short succession of wardrobe mistresses, from Francesca de Warre – I've always thought she must originally have spelt her name Dewar, though she does look voluptuously continental so I may be wrong – through the glamorous Jane Westwater and, culminating in the second season, in the best of the lot of them. Mrs Marshall stayed till the company closed in 1965 and spent much of her life in dressing room four slaving over a hot sewing machine worked by a treadle and listening sympathetically to the romantic entanglements of a succession of young actresses and never letting dab about any of them. Bless her, Alice Marshall was worth her weight in gold to the Company. Simple, straightforward, benign, she saw no evil in anyone, loved us all and brought an enormous amount of common sense to all our doings. No terrible anguish of the heart couldn't be assuaged with a comforting and sympathetically banal word, no intense crisis over missing or wrongly shaped costumes couldn't be instantly righted without a philosophical "Och, let me sort it" and a turn to the sewing machine.

Dressing rooms five, six and seven are to the left. Five is a smallish room which won't accommodate more than three normal-sized actors in comfort and is to be my home for much of the next seven years. Six is a bigger room and holds more actors while the last one, seven, is the stage management room where the ASMs who play small parts – and all of them do at one time or another – usually change and make up.

And that was the building as we found it that mid-September morning when we came in singly from the tram stop in the middle of Leith Walk opposite those doors and under the Roller-Skating sign, across the silent and deserted foyer, through the doors into the dark auditorium and saw ahead of us over the backs of the empty seats the dim and unadorned stage, shadowy in the single working light, waiting enigmatically to receive us.

CHAPTER TWO

Curtain Going Up And Nearly Coming Down Again

I have to be very careful with rose-coloured spectacles. They're deceptively pleasant things, and at this distance of time when your eyesight's not as good as it used to be and you don't want your spectacles broken, you tend to remember everything as being fun and warm and happy. I'm quite sure most of it was, but it was also life and life which is nothing but fun and warmth and happiness is probably a bit dull. There has to be a leavening.

But fun and warmth and happiness is the prevailing impression left by the passage of the years. It was also stimulating and educational – I learnt more about the business at the Gateway than at any other period of my career and I suppose it's true that you learn more quickly and better if you're happy than if you're thoroughly miserable. Over the last few weeks, though, I've thought about those days a lot more deeply and dispassionately and many of the memories have become clearer than the usual rosy ones which are always in the back of my head, and there are nasty bits. Only a few but I'll try to report them accurately. But if you have tears, don't prepare to shed them yet.

We gathered on the stage, clutching our scripts. There was a motley assortment of battered old chairs arranged in a half moon round a central table with three chairs with their backs to the auditorium facing the half moon. There were papers and ashtrays on the table and the model of a set, most of the normal paraphernalia of a first rehearsal in a repertory theatre. And stilted conversation. "Hallo . . . I don't think we've met . . ." Gradually numbers increased. The stilted conversation grew less stilted, there was the odd laugh relieving the tension, tentative introductions were made. And standing by the table, hands in pockets, a cigarette hanging between his lips, an ashtray already reasonably full in front of him, stood Gibbie, looking more like a benign gnome than ever. At last he seemed satisfied that the muster was complete, and he clapped his hands.

"Good morning," he said.

"Good morning, Gibbie," we dutifully replied.

"We'll go on with the introductions while we take the brew of the bean of Brazil. Then we'll start the read through."

Young female acolytes or ASMs came through from the backstage corridor bearing a tray with a vast kettle on it, a tin of coffee, numerous battered and chipped old cups and mugs, a packet of sugar and a pint bottle of milk. There was never much ceremony about the coffee break at the Gateway. The most important thing was to get the stuff and get it fast. They put it on the table and we were invited to help ourselves. We did so. Gibbie watched disapprovingly as some of us added milk.

"Robbing the wee calves of their birthright," he muttered.

It's all a bit of a blur. Too many new impressions to take in at the same time, but after a quarter of an hour or so, there was a clap of the hands from Gibbie.

"Gurgle, gurgle, doon the thrapple," he said. "We're not here to enjoy ourselves."

32

The tray with its empty cups and mugs was taken away and people began to open scripts and distribute themselves along the half moon of seats. Gibbie set fire to yet another cigarette and sat down at the centre of the table.

"Everyone settled? Right. Ready, steady, go."

My part didn't start until much later so for the first half hour or so I was free to watch and listen, to take in these new faces and hear these new voices. Not all new. Tom and Lennox I'd recently met. Gibbie I already knew. I'd known Ian MacNaughton, a tall, dark gangling young man, since my early days at RADA, and he'd been in the Citizens' Company too. He stayed at the Gateway for that first season, later he was to become the producer of *Monty Python's Flying Circus* and later still he disappeared into the wilds of Germany and never reappeared. I don't know what happened to him and I can't find anyone who does.*
He never did me any harm but one of my misfortunes that season was that I had to share dressing room five with him and the thing I remember best is that he used to pee in the washbasin. I'd never shared a dressing room with him at the Citizens' so I was unaware of this aberration in his character. The first time it happened I protested – Did he mind? I had to wash my face in that, but his only response was, "It's all right. I always turn the tap on." No one else ever did that as far as I'm aware – peed in the basin, I mean, not turned the tap on – and it seemed the height of selfishness and laziness, especially as there was a perfectly serviceable loo ten yards along the corridor. There. That's the first of the unpleasantnesses out of the way.

There were other people who were new to me. Our stage manager, sitting next to Gibbie. Jonny Lee. Hair like a hearth brush, squat, masculine in voice and movement and strong as a stage manager has to be, she was to stay in her post for two seasons. Married to and divorced from Miles Lee who ran a puppet theatre in Edinburgh, Jonny was a frenetic soul, loud and boisterous, who had two great

---

*Ian died in Munich in December 2002

phrases. "Fegs-alearie" was the one which expressed mild wonder. The other, which indicated astonishment or disbelief, was "Fech ma danglers". I don't know where she got them from, I'm not sure about the spelling, and I'm definitely dubious about their basic implications, but I've never heard them anywhere else except as an echo of Jonny herself. She'd worked at the Gateway before for Sadie Aitken so she knew all the theatre's idiosyncrasies. She was a good friend but a bad enemy and she took dislikes to people, usually ASMs, for reasons which were difficult to fathom. It had already started, though I wasn't aware of it this early in the Company's life. One of the ASMs, Margaret Hilder, had already fallen foul of Jonny somehow and was not to be released from her grip until the end of the season and she never reappeared. The other ASM, Kathryn Orr, was playing a small part and seemed to earn Jonny's approval.

Sheila Prentice, the juvenile, was fresh from the new Glasgow College of Music and Drama which Gibbie in later years, after we'd received many ex-students from its doors, referred to as the "Actors' Factory". He also rechristened her "Tingle-Puss". She stayed for the season and part of the next but during the later one we became aware of a young man who began to haunt dressing room three. He was apparently an upcoming singer and comedian who had been a fellow-student. Tingle-Puss gave up the business to marry Andy Stewart. Thereafter she disappeared from the working stage. Since over the coming years she produced six children that was hardly surprising.

John Young, or Jungle as Gibbie quickly christened him. Dear John. A marvellous friend, husband of Freddie who later became my agent, and father of Paul who followed his father's footsteps into the theatre and was to start his professional career at the Gateway later that year as Tiny Tim in *A Christmas Carol*. Kind and gentle, John had the most ungovernable twinkle and could convulse you in the middle of a scene just by raising an eyebrow. He had started his career before the war, seen service throughout it and learnt his craft in the hard grind of weekly rep in England before coming home to Scotland, where the transfer to fortnightly rep was something of a doddle.

And then there was George Davies. George was possibly a little younger than Gibbie which meant he must have been about sixty at this time. He had an india-rubber face and india-rubber legs and the most lugubrious expression you ever saw which made him ideal for comic funeral scenes. He also had a bald head. At the dress rehearsal of one play George came into the wings before the start and said to Gibbie: "Jimmy, I just don't know what to do with my hair for this part." And of course Gibbie pounced. "Well, if I were you," he said caustically, "I'd part *that* one *that* way and *that* one the *other* way." George had worked on the railways in an administrative capacity all his life but had followed his real love into the amateur theatre as a hobby and into occasional sound broadcasts for the BBC, because in his younger day that was all that was available. George was very happily married to Jenny, they had two sons and a daughter and they needed the steady secure income the railway unstimulatingly provided. A year or so short of retiring age George had a heart attack and was forced to give up work. Robert Kemp, who had known him for years, went to see him in hospital during the summer of 1953 and told him about the new company which was being formed. From his sick bed George pricked up his ears. That was what Robert had been waiting for and rather hesitantly, because he didn't really know how George's future health was going to be, asked if he would be interested in joining the Gateway Company now that the daily grind of the railway was willy-nilly behind him. Without hesitation George said yes. It fulfilled his life's ambition and he joined us. As Jenny confirmed later it made a new man of him. He worked with the Company for the next six years and enjoyed better health than he had experienced throughout most of his life, turning in a series of richly comic and sometimes very moving performances. There are stories about George nearly as plentiful as the stories about Gibbie and I'll try to remember them as we go along.

Marjorie Dalziel had been with the Scottish National Players and had also been one of the leading characters in the celebrated radio series *The McFlannels*. She had married her professor at university, George Dalziel, who was very much older than she was. Marjorie was with the Company as a sort of second leading lady to Lennox. I think she felt that on some occasions she should be leading and Lennox following and I don't think her time at the Gateway was as happy as it was for most of the rest of us.

Sitting at the table beside Gibbie and Jonny was a tall, thin, worried-looking dark-haired lady with spectacles and a permanently confused expression which didn't necessarily reflect her true state of mind. Her conversation took place in an endless minor key and even a mildly light-hearted story was delivered in tones of abject tragedy. This was the legendary Molly McEwen, who had a huge and thoroughly deserved reputation not only in Scotland but also south of the border as a stage designer. For this season and for the next two she was the principal designer for the Company and with her assistant, Peter Norris, she produced some staggering sets with the utmost economy and inventiveness, working in a succession of freezing cold and dilapidated hovels in run-down areas of the town, because the one thing the Gateway didn't have was an in-house scene store and workshop. It was one of the Company's insoluble headaches that new sets had to be brought in by lorry late on changeover Saturday nights or early on Sunday mornings while the old set was being dismantled and then driven away to the current igloo for recycling. Molly also designed the costumes. At the Gateway this didn't mean making them because that was too time-consuming and too expensive. But she'd arrange their hire, design alterations to existing costumes borrowed from Sadie's wardrobe, and always the finished result was breathtaking in its aptness.

Ah. Sadie's wardrobe Excuse me while I go off at a brief tangent here, but I have to give warm credit to Sadie and her wardrobe. Not just her wardrobe, but her stock of props as well. Sadie was a veritable cornucopia. Down the south corridor which stretched through from the foyer to backstage in the same way as the tea-room and kitchen did on the north side was a treasury of cupboards on the ground floor which contained Sadie's wardrobe and props, accumulated over many years from many amateur productions and from many sources. Upstairs, on the same level as our dressing rooms there were flats and fireplaces, windows and doors, bits of staircases and banisters, statues and plinths and balconies, cut out trees and ground rows of low hills, with still more props which might come in useful some day, from fishbowls to fake flowers, from Victorian umbrellas to Grecian urns, from stuffed parrots to gilded birdcages. You wanted an exotic prop or an out of the way costume? Ask Sadie. If she didn't have it on the premises she'd know where to find it. Sadie saved the life of many a desperate ASM. Okay? End of tangent. Back to our first meeting.

Who else? The statuesque Francesca de Warre, of course. She was there. And Kenneth Miles, expertly groomed, not a hair out of place, immaculate in a blazer and perfectly pressed grey slacks. For this occasion he had deserted the Company Manager's office, where he had left his secretary, Margaret Mackintosh, to deal with the telephone and the correspondence.

James Roughead, a Scots actor based in London, had joined the Company for this one production. I never really got to know him well, and he only appeared in occasional productions with the Company at odd times later and most of them were ones I wasn't in.

I think you've met everyone now and it might be a good idea to imprint them firmly on your mind, because not all of this Company lasted into the second or subsequent seasons.

Rehearsals for the opening production proceeded in exactly the same way as rehearsals for any fortnightly repertory theatre production. After the read-through was over there was discussion about character and the play and how we were going to tackle it, then an adjournment to the Windsor Buffet for lunch, liquid or solid, take your pick. The Windsor was, until very recently, a lovely old-fashioned pub. At this time it was privately owned so that it escaped the depredations of the breweries' architectural vandals, and we generally found a table in one of the many odd corners. The place was always full by the time we got there. There was the regular drinking clientèle and there were many local shopkeepers having a quick lunch. We got to know them all and they accepted us as part of their lives with great kindness, and every day there were some if not all of the cheerful Muirs pulling pints behind the counter and always ready with a laugh and a joke. The pub's spam fritters were a delight, but they were only on on a Friday.

And our way of working was established right then and remained with only minor variations throughout my time at the Gateway. We'd done the read-through. The next morning we'd block the first act. This was slow. Inching round the stage at the orders of the producer, noses buried in scripts, pencil frantically making a scribble to show where you had to move at a particular point, and always the prayer that you'd be able to decipher it when you came to study the part in the privacy of your own home in the afternoon. This went on for most of the first week and by the Friday or the Saturday the script was being tentatively laid aside and without that crutch to lean on you were feeling very vulnerable. This was the agonising time as you tried to coax words out of the air where they seemed to flutter shyly just out of reach. And the moves. Where should I be? Was it down here or up there? And you'd all get strung out across the stage in a straight line and a croaky voice would come out of the darkened auditorium:

"Look at you! It's like *Iolanthe* at Cowdenbeath!"

This was also the agonising time for the ASM on the book. To prompt or not to prompt. That was the inevitable question. Whatever she did would be wrong. Don't prompt, that was a pause, for God's sake. Prompt, are you asleep? George was the one who created most agonies, mainly for himself. "Don't tell me. . .! *Don't tell me* . . .! Er – What is it? Oh, aye, that's enough. I know it now . . . What is it again. . .? I don't know what's wrong with me. I knew it fine round the fire with Jenny last night." Then the second week. Smoother. The words coming more easily. A shape building. So that by the Saturday you could see the product properly cooked and almost ready to be eaten by the audience on the Monday night. Then start again with the next play on Tuesday and the whole rigmarole is re-enacted.

As this was the opening production and therefore pretty important, and as the play was revived later as a New Year show, and as it's disappeared into the mists of time and hardly anyone's heard of it nowadays I'd better say a bit more about it than I will about most of the productions we did. To those who don't know *The Forrigan Reel*, which is a rather minor Bridie, the story is set mainly in the eighteenth century and mainly in a big house and grounds in the Highlands. There are several versions of it, including one with songs, but the one we did was the earliest and arguably the best. The plot is somewhat complex – it's Bridie, after all – but basically it concerns the wife of the local laird, Mrs Grant of Forrigan, who has been struck with a mysterious illness and thinks she's a clock. Eminent physicians are powerless to effect a cure and she can't stop walking around going tick-tock and occasionally striking the hour. On the estate live Old MacAlpine, who is an expert fiddler, and Donald MacAlpine, his son, who has pretensions as a Highland dancer. They eventually cure Mrs Grant by forcing her to dance through the night with Donald while Old MacAlpine plays the fiddle for them and by the morning Mrs Grant is miraculously cured. The MacAlpines set up a sort of eighteenth century practice for curing people with similar psychosomatic disorders and make a lot of money.

All right, it sounds quite amusing, and some of it is hilarious, occasionally unconsciously so. Every performance when it came time for the dance, George Davies as Old MacAlpine would pick up his fiddle and arrange it under his chin. That in itself and preparing his bow took about five minutes' worth of business. Just offstage from where George was sitting, the real fiddler was stationed behind a wing piece ready to start. Finally, having milked every laugh he could, George turned towards the fiddler in the wings, gave him a down beat with his bow, said "Now!" as though he were the starter on a race-track and away the pair of them would go into the Forrigan Reel.

On the first night we met the Goblins. Now the Goblins were an integral part of the Gateway. They were our regular scene shifters, and they were both small, which may explain how they got their name in the first place. One of them was thin and known as Jimmy and the other one was stout and known as Jimmy Gob to distinguish them. But they were always known collectively as the Goblins. They were a marvellous pair. They worked for the Corporation Cleansing Department during the day and came in to shift scenery at night for plays that required a change of set and to dismantle and construct the old and new sets on changeover weekends. Things seemed to fall off the backs of lorries whenever the Goblins were around. You got unlabelled bottles of whisky and such like luxuries which were still in short supply thrust into your hand in the darkness of the wings just as you were about to make an entrance, accompanied by a hoarse whisper: "Only ten bob to you, Mickey." But they were intensely proud of their work and were always concerned that *their* productions should run without a hitch. There was one night when a cleat came loose and the flat it was supposed to be attached to started swaying dangerously just as the curtain went up. The Goblins, sacrificing the chance to get into the backstage corridor for a fag, stood resolutely holding it upright and unmoving until the curtain came down again about half an hour later. They were extremely efficient except on the day when Hearts won the cup. The chaos which reigned backstage that night must have been as great as that on the pitch at the final whistle in the afternoon and I don't know how Jonny and her staff got through that performance without a major disaster. All I know is that there seemed to be collapsed Goblins, mercifully silent, not even snoring, all over the wings.

The Forrigan Reel was fun to do, the audiences were good and they seemed to enjoy it and it looked as if the company had got off to a healthy start.

The day after we'd opened there was general satisfaction at what we'd achieved, the notices had been good and should help to draw people to this new venture half-way down Leith Walk, and the stage was cleared for rehearsals of the second play, J B Priestley's *An Inspector Calls*.

Now as with Kipling's tribal lays there are nine and sixty ways of doing the play. This was to be my third time in it. I'd done it in my very early RADA days when the producer had been unwise enough to cast me as the Inspector. An additional misfortune was that she had *ideas* about how the play was to be done. The Inspector was not of this world, divorced from the rest of the characters, she said. You couldn't fault the reasoning, but she felt that he had to be so isolated that he must never come into physical contact with anyone, never shake hands, never touch an article of furniture, never sit down, never even open or close a door for himself, which was fine in theory but very tiring on the feet. In fact I wondered, granting this premise, how you could justify allowing your feet to touch the floor, but there didn't seem to be any alternative to that. And who had been playing

Mr Birling in that production? Ian MacNaughton. A little later I'd done it at the Byre. This time I'd played Eric, the young son who gets the girl into real trouble. We had another producer stretching his wings of imagination: we played it in a set of black drapes and at the back of the stage there was a special picture of a factory pinned to one of the black curtains. During Mr Birling's long speech about how good times were in the manufacturing industry so long as the workpeople were kept in their place and how we were in for a period of prosperity and scientific advance, look at the new liner they were building, the *Titanic*, it was unsinkable and of course there wasn't going to be a war, this factory would light up as if it were burning. Symbolic and significant but looking a bit odd suspended all alone on a blank black curtain. The play seems to attract this sort of productional self-indulgence, where eager producers feel they can help to improve the text by investing it with their own whims as witness the recent rendering of it where the entire set got destroyed at every performance. You can't go much further than that. And I don't think it's necessary. The play is perfectly capable of standing on its own feet quite naturally and telling its own story. Fortunately Gibbie was an intensely practical producer who believed in letting the play speak for itself. There was nothing symbolic about our production. He allowed the dichotomy between the family and the inspector to find its own way and it was very effective because of that. Mind you, it did create problems. *The Glasgow Herald* was obviously short of critics that particular opening Monday night and they must have sent the office boy. The review appeared in Tuesday's edition, and complained that Mr Priestley clearly didn't know very much about police procedure because if his inspector had been a real policeman he would undoubtedly have been drummed out of the force for the way he handled the case. Heigh-ho, your life in their hands.

I played Eric again and Sheila Prentice played the Birling daughter

Sheila. One evening we reached the third act and we Birlings were discussing the recently departed inspector and suspicions were growing that he wasn't really all he seemed, when I noticed that Tingle-Puss wasn't in her normal position downstage left by the prompt corner. She was moving upstage centre. I thought with some indignation that this was an unusual way of attracting the limelight. Where on earth did she think she was going? I watched her draw to a halt behind a large armchair. Once she was there she gave a sudden shimmy, stepped away from the chair and returned to her normal position, leaving a little mound of white material behind out of sight of the audience. She told us afterwards that her petticoat had worked loose and it was the best way she could think of for getting rid of it without attracting attention.

An Inspector Calls, set in the English Midlands, proved to the audiences that though the company might be primarily concerned with presenting Scottish plays they were capable of a wider appeal.

And we were learning about our producer. During his spell at the Gateway, and even before, Gibbie had a plethora of the most individual remarks which let you know immediately what was in his mind.

"Get upstage of the door so that you can let her get off the set, otherwise there'll be a bus accident."

He was getting a bit deaf. In ordinary conversation he would occasionally cup his ear, look pained and command:

"Speak up! You're not on the stage now!"

At a crowded party Gibbie would come in, look for a seat, find them all occupied, and would say loudly and philosophically:

"The young ones sit and the old ones stand."

The phrases form a rich leitmotif for the Gateway days and they continued long afterwards. I'm afraid they lose much of their pith presenting them on the printed page: they need that rich, croaky, couthy Scots voice to bring out the full effect, but I can't resist a couple more. Some years after The Edinburgh Gateway Company closed I met Gibbie on the platform at Queen Street Station in Glasgow. I hadn't seen him for some time, so I said:

"Are you busy, Gibbie?"

"Oh, not very," he said. "I'm doing this television play for the BB guess the third letter, then I'm going into the Citizens' play at the Festicle – " he always referred to the Edinburgh International Festival as the Festicle – " and then I've got a wee wireless in London. After that," he said with an air of great finality, "I've got nothing. I'm going to retire. I'm going to lie on silken cushions, read glossy magazines and finger gilt ornaments."

It was the way the phrase came out with absolute fluency as though he'd been rehearsing it for weeks. Maybe he had.

Gibbie was a fairly benevolent producer but he had his own high standards and he expected you to match them. If the run-through of an act had not gone as well as it should have done he would come down to the edge of the steps and look up at us all, spectacles glinting in the working light, cigarette in mouth and an ashtray in his hand because the auditorium had already been cleaned for the evening show.

"That wasn't very good, was it?" he'd say.

"No, Gibbie," we'd reply meekly.

"Right. Then we'll do the whole *sordid* thing again."

The "sordid thing" could be anything from an act which had to be re-rehearsed to an indigestible meal which had to be eaten or an extremely bad play which had to be sat through.

After *An Inspector Calls* we returned to the Scottish theme with J M Barrie's *What Every Woman Knows*. Barrie had been out of fashion for some time – apart from the perennial *Peter Pan*, of course – and perhaps there was something of a risk in presenting him. *What Every Woman Knows* was not so well-known as *Mary Rose* or *Dear Brutus*, and was probably not so well constructed overall, though it had what is claimed to be the best first act of a full-length play written in the past century. In this act – and it almost stands as a play on its own – John Shand, an impoverished student at the university, breaks into the Wylies' house in order to read the books they have and which he himself can't afford to buy for his studies. He is caught by the Wylies: father Alick and his two sons David and James and the reason for the break-in becomes clear. The Wylies have a dearly beloved sister, Maggie, who unfortunately has failed to find a husband because, as she says of herself, she lacks charm and she's now getting on a bit. Her menfolk devise a plan whereby they will allow John use of their books and provide him with a sum of £300 to complete his studies on condition that in five years time when he has graduated as a minister, if Maggie is still unmarried, he will take her as his wife. The bargain is sealed. On the first night, at the sealing, whisky was poured and George Davies, playing Alick Wylie took a mouthful of the diluted gravy browning doing duty as whisky, spluttered and said indignantly, "Gey wersh!"

If you're wanting to make a lot of money the last thing you do is start a fortnightly repertory company. There is no easier way to lose a fortune and no more difficult way to make one. And the Gateway was situated down Leith Walk, not in the conventional, fashionable entertainment triangle of the Lyceum Theatre, where the Wilson Barrett Company was still recycling past West End successes, the Usher Hall, where the Scottish National Orchestra presented classical concerts to dinner-jacketed and evening-gowned society, and the King's Theatre where pre-London tours were tried out and post-London tours mopped up a little additional gravy. We had a grant from the Arts Council, but only a small one because the Arts Council had many calls on its limited purse and they expected us at least to pull our weight at the box office. The most we could hope for was to keep our heads above water and in fact we seemed to be doing that. Yet the board of directors, who were no fools and knew the ways of the theatre, were well aware that we were still in the part of the year where things were fairly cheerful, but that once we were over the hump of the New Year we reached the dead time when the nights were very long, the days were very cold and people tended to stay indoors and listen to their wirelesses rather than risk breaking their ankles on icy pavements. (The wireless had not yet become the radio and so far there wasn't all that much television, but it was coming). It was necessary to accumulate feathers for the nest while we could in order that there might be sufficient warmth to see us through to the end of the season in March.

What Every Woman Knows was followed by Robert Kemp's story of Robert Burns's affair with Nancy Maclehose during his visit to Edinburgh. Called *The Other Dear Charmer* it starred Iris Russell as Nancy with Tom playing Burns. I had the minor part of Burns's friend, Robert Ainslie.

When the costumes arrived I found I had been issued with a coat, waistcoat and breeches, a pair of stockings and buckled shoes. I had to face the problem which is endemic amongst actors: how do you keep your stockings up? I'd tried belts and braces and pennies and string and bandages like tourniquets round my thighs and none of these stopped the damned things from wrinkling in an unsightly manner and ending up round your ankles by the end of the act. Eventually Sheila suggested a suspender belt: after all, they worked for girls, why shouldn't one work for me? I told her she was brilliant – again – and would she go into Binns to buy me one? She was slightly embarrassed at the idea of doing this, but I told her it was her idea in the first place and she wouldn't be nearly so embarrassed as I would be having to do it for myself, so she relented. Her story of this escapade is worth recording.

She went up to the underwear counter and told the assistant she wanted to buy a suspender belt.

"Yes, madam," said the assistant, reaching for her tape measure.

"It's all right. I know the size," said Sheila hastily. "Thirty six."

The assistant looked at her very trim waist and laughed indulgently.

"Oh, dear me, madam, I don't think you need anything as big as that," she said.

By now covered in embarrassment Sheila blurted out:

"No, it's not for me, it's for my husband."

What sort of husband the assistant thought she had isn't revealed.

One night during the run I was standing at the washbasin after the performance stripped to my underpants, washing. I'm not sure whether I still had the size thirty six suspender belt on or not, but I hope not . . . Tom, with whom I shared dressing room five, had already washed, changed and hurried off somewhere. There was a knock at the door. I removed my soapy hands from my face and spluttered permission to enter. The door opened and an immensely tall stranger poked his head in and looked round.

"Mr Fleming?" asked the stranger who wasn't really a stranger, though I'd never met him, but then everyone recognised Tyrone Guthrie.

"He's gone," I said, awestruck and embarrassed by my state of deshabille.

"Oh," he said, disappointed. "How do you do? My name's Guthrie. Enjoyed the show. Wish I could have seen more of you."

And the face withdrew before I could grab any covering garments in case his wish was fulfilled.

While *The Other Dear Charmer* was playing, N C Hunter's Czechovian comedy *A Day By The Sea* came for a week to the King's Theatre during a post-London tour. It had an all-star cast and I think it was Sadie who, knowing two of the stars, thought it would be a good publicity stunt for us to get them to come and visit us during rehearsal and have a cup of coffee. So one morning there was an unusual brew of the bean of Brazil because not only did it come out of china cups and saucers lent by Sadie from her props cupboard, but there were also what Gibbie described as chocky-wocky-bicky-poohs. There arrived to partake of all this Sir Lewis Casson and Dame Sybil Thorndike. There is a photograph of the occasion from *The Evening Dispatch* in my press cuttings book. There we all are, in our best shirts, ties and jackets, looking surprisingly trim and neat as if we'd stepped out of *The Tailor and Cutter* – or perhaps been pushed out of it – surrounding these two legends of the theatre. It's one of my clearest recollections. They weren't nearly as physically big as their reputations and stage personae had led us to believe. In fact they looked quite ordinary, and their conversation was certainly so. Both of them were well into their seventies by this time, but the energy and enthusiasm and sheer warmth which poured from them, especially from Dame Sybil, because Sir Lewis always allowed himself to be overshadowed by his wife, was almost palpable. Dame Sybil spoke of the fact that they both had so much still to learn about the business and Sir Lewis speculated wonderingly on what it must be like to be a big star. It wasn't an act. It was most sincerely meant.

The Other Dear Charmer was followed by an adaptation of *A Christmas Carol* featuring Ian MacNaughton as Ebenezer Scrooge, a part for which he was physically ideal, and it drew good festive audiences. What the Gateway Council was looking for now was a New Year winner and they'd found it: Graham Moffat's *Bunty Pulls the Strings*, which had first been staged in 1911 and had run for over 600 performances in London. No one has ever quite understood why this very Scottish kailyard comedy should prove so popular in the West End but it was. It may have been a happy combination of expatriate Scots nostalgically renewing their youth and curious English wondering how on earth this strange race lived in the not so distant past but very distant north amongst all that snow and woad. Whatever it was, people queued for seats and the House Full notices were out for nearly two years. There were those on the so-called artistic fringe of Edinburgh who held up their hands in horror at the idea of what was already by then the leading Scottish repertory theatre prostituting itself with rubbish like this, but the venture was unashamedly commercial, and those who put forward the idea that *Bunty* was artistically worthless actually exposed themselves as pretty narrow-minded. It's very charming, very – terrible word – pawky, it's exactly how the Scots seem to think of themselves in some long-lost Utopia. It had not been performed professionally in Edinburgh for many years and when we did it at the Gateway it was planned for a four week run. But the advance bookings were so good – Sadie had obviously been working overtime on her Women's Rural Institute secretaries – that the Council took a collective deep breath and extended it by a week. Our production had the inestimable advantage of having the lovely Rona Anderson playing Bunty Biggar, the managing young woman everyone loved and admired. "All my plans is working splendid," says Bunty to herself as she pulls the strings at the ends of which all the other characters dance. Rona had played the part a year or two before at the Citizens' and she was an Edinburgh girl, now married to Gordon Jackson, so she was coming home in two different ways.

Bunty was a delight to perform. It was easy playing, bright and lively, Gibbie was exactly the right producer for this type of play and there was nothing more enjoyable than walking on to the stage every night – and twice on Wednesdays and Saturdays – to be greeted by constant gales of laughter from packed houses. As Weelum Sprunt, Bunty's long-suffering fiancé, I had the last line as I took Bunty in my arms, heard her telling me that when we were married she would go on ordering me around, she couldn't help herself, and I said I didn't care, I would just glory in my shame and it was a joy to hear the cheers of delight as the final curtain came down.

For me *A Christmas Carol* and *Bunty Pulls the Strings* were particularly enjoyable because Sheila was in them too. This was the first time we'd worked together on the stage since the Fraser Neal Players in the summer of 1952. She had begun to carve out a very useful career for herself in BBC radio. At that time there was a lot of radio. Besides Saturday Night Theatres, serials, single plays, Children's Hours and many dramatised documentaries there were at least five dramatised school programmes every week during the school term for which you got paid three pounds ten shillings. A pittance by today's levels but it was quite a good fee in those days, especially if you could get two or three broadcasts a week which was not at all unusual. Sheila had taken a radio audition a year or two before in Dundee of all places but nothing had come of it and it was Madeleine Christie who suggested she took another one in Glasgow and concentrated on playing small boys because Scottish BBC radio's permanent "boy", Elsie Payne, had recently died and they were desperate to find a replacement. She duly took the audition in Glasgow with the head of Radio Drama, James Crampsey, and passed as she had passed the previous one. But there was a difference this time. Within a week or so she got her first offer. It came from a Schools Producer in Edinburgh, a nice man but a humourless wonder, and the letter started "Dear Miss Donald, I hear from Mr Crampsey that you do small boys", which was not perhaps the most encouraging introduction to the medium. She had by *Christmas Carol* and *Bunty* time, however, done several small boys at different stages of pre-pubescence. All these programmes went out live in those days, so during the school holidays they came to a stop and now she got the chance to come back to the stage. She played a batty spinster aunt in *Carol* and a gossipy old woman, Maggie Mercer in the kirkyard scene in *Bunty*, the sort of parts she began to make her own and which she is still playing with even greater panache and authority fifty years later.

But it wasn't all smooth. On the Friday night of the fourth week John Young, playing Bunty's father Tammas Biggar, was sitting at the kitchen table on the stage towards the end of the third act. When it came to the point where he had to get up and go offstage, he found himself locked in place, unable to move. John had suffered from a bad back for some time and was to be troubled by it with increasing pain and discomfort for the rest of his life. By some superhuman effort he managed to get from the table to the door in the set, bent like an upturned capital L. Those of us on the stage and in the wings could see he was in trouble but of course the audience didn't and they thought this was exceptionally funny business, though maybe a little over the top, and they roared with appreciative laughter as he made his painful exit. In those days it was called lumbago. They've got a fancier name for it now and physiotherapists can do marvels for mobility and the easement of pain but those remedies weren't available then. The only treatment was bed rest. Fortunately it was John's last exit and he managed to get on to the stage to take his bow, already bent into the appropriate attitude, and then he was carefully taken home and put to bed. He was confined there next day while Gibbie hastily mugged up the lines and went on for the Saturday matinée and for the evening show. He was word perfect, as Gibbie almost always was, but then he'd produced the play and had actually played Tammas in the Citizens' production with Rona, so he was merely revising an old part.

By this time the Company were almost a week into rehearsals for the next production which was to be a new play by Albert Mackie, a well known Edinburgh journalist probably best remembered as MacNib for his little daily verses in *The Evening Dispatch*. His play was a cosy local comedy called *Hame*. Now there was already a sort of semi-officially established practice of allowing each permanent member of the Company one production off in the season. Did that mean a fortnight's paid holiday, I hear you ask? Nothing so grand, because although you would be free of rehearsals during the day for the play you weren't in you'd still be playing at night and when the play you weren't in went on and you got your nights free you would be starting rehearsals for the next one during the day, so although *Hame* was my play off any idea of heading away for the south of France or the Bahamas or even Elie was out.

As I said the news about John wasn't too good on that Saturday morning. He was still confined to bed unable to move with any degree of freedom. Rehearsals for *Hame* were continuing in spite of Gibbie having to go on that afternoon to play Tammas. Kenneth Miles rang me and asked if I would stand in for John, at least for rehearsals, in the hope that rest would make things better quickly. Of course I agreed: Sheila and I hadn't yet booked the tickets to the south of France and I went in for what was my first rehearsal while everyone else had been at it for nearly a week. If the worst came to the worst and I had to go on on the first night a week on Monday I would have a lot of serious catching-up to do. Missing a free Saturday morning wasn't too bad, because I'd have to be in the theatre for the matinée and the evening show anyway.

It was a heavier Saturday than I'd expected, however, and I couldn't spend the Sunday learning the lines which would have been ideal, because I'd been booked to do a broadcast at the BBC in Queen Street. This took all day with an evening transmission so it was late before I got home and back to the lines. Sheila told me that the latest bulletin from John's bedside, while better, didn't give cause for a huge amount of optimism about his imminent return, so I was back in to the Gateway to rehearse on the Monday morning.

I don't know whether it was the added pressure of all this, but I felt incredibly tired that morning. I told myself that this was quite natural after a particularly heavy weekend, but at the same time my head seemed to spin occasionally and my legs felt as if they were made of water and there were times when my balance seemed suspect. It didn't get any better as the morning progressed and by the time we'd come to the brew of the bean of Brazil I was feeling decidedly woozy. We gurgle, gurgled down the thrapple and resumed rehearsal. I wondered if I should say anything, but we had enough trouble with John's incapacity and I decided not to. It would all clear up, no doubt. I was sitting in a rehearsal chair, reading from the script, guiltily feeling that I should have learnt it by now, with the others in the cast round about, without scripts, lines learnt, when suddenly everything swirled inside my head, I felt myself getting to my feet, and heard a cry which came from me. I sounded as though I were a long way away from myself. And then, in the well-known phrase, everything went black.

The next thing I was aware of was a bell ringing very closely in my head. As I pulled myself up through deep water and surfaced groggily I began to realise that it wasn't actually in my head but was certainly all around it, that it was an ambulance bell and I was in the damned thing. It stopped – the ambulance and the bell – and I heard the doors open, there was a lot of manoeuvring and people running hither and thither and whatever I was lying on was lifted and jerked around a bit. I didn't care. I was quite content to lie there and let other people do the work. I'd forgotten temporarily about the rehearsal which I must so abruptly have left and a great lassitude swept over me. It's a good word, lassitude. I rather liked it at that point and I let it wander round inside my head and I closed my eyes thinking it'll all sort itself out in a minute.

After lassitude had wandered into oblivion again I woke up properly in bed in a hospital ward and there was a nurse and a short, grim-looking man with a large moustache and militant eyebrows looking sternly down at me as if he'd caught me eating peas with my knife. Later I came to know him as John Halliday-Croome, the diabetic specialist at the Royal Infirmary of Edinburgh.

I'd contracted diabetes when I was twelve years old. In other words I'd had it for ten years and during that time I'd never had any trouble with it. In fact I'd almost come to forget about it. That was my big mistake. You can't do that with diabetes, especially if you're on insulin. The best you can do is live with it in a state of armed neutrality, aware of its power over you, but not submitting to it. Over a long time I probably hadn't been sufficiently aware of what was happening inside me, but frankly I'd been working almost every day in life for the past two years and very happy and grateful for being able to do so, but this was the crunch.

As I lay there warily I didn't know what they'd done to me since I'd arrived unexpectedly on their doorstep, but I examined myself mentally all over and felt all right. Mind you, what I would have felt like if I'd tried to stand up I don't know but I wasn't given the chance to find out.

"I'm terribly sorry to have been a nuisance," I said. "Thank you for what you've done. I'll get back to work now."

Dr Halliday-Croome fixed me with a beady eye which he was to do for many years thereafter. It was almost as though he were blaming me for having diabetes, but I realise now that he was probably just blaming me for not taking more care of myself.

"Where do you think you're going?" he demanded.

"Back to rehearsal," I said. "What's the time?"

The nurse looked at her watch.

"Half past two," she said.

I blinked.

"It can't be," I said. "Rehearsal will be over."

They said nothing.

"I've got a show to do tonight," I said helpfully to put them fully in the picture, but my voice quavered a little because this uncompromising attitude wasn't exactly encouraging.

"You'll be doing no show tonight," said Dr Halliday-Croome. "In fact you won't be doing any shows this week."

"But – but – " I said, and went on saying it. By the time of the third but he was already half way down the ward towards the escape hatch, followed by the nurse.

Later Sheila was allowed to come in and see me and bring me pyjamas and things. There's something very final about pyjamas in those circumstances. It means that you're becoming a permanent part of the scenery. I complained to her in panic that they were incarcerating me in here, the Gestapo would be guarding the doors and they weren't going to let me out to do the show.

"I know," she said.

"But – but – " I said again. At least she stayed where she was so I was able to formulate a question or two to follow. "Who's going to play Weelum tonight then?" I asked triumphantly. That, I felt, was the unanswerable question. We didn't have understudies. I had to be there.

"Gibbie."

"But Gibbie's going on for John. Not even Gibbie can do both."

"John's back."

"I know. It's John's back that's caused all the trouble."

"No, he's back playing Tammas."

This was all getting too much for me in my delicate state and Sheila began the business of neatly arranging sheets and pillows which is always a bad sign.

"Now you're not to worry or you'll make yourself worse. We've got to get you right and make sure this doesn't happen again."

I sank back on the newly plumped pillows. Aghast, that's what I was. Had I given my last performance of Weelum Sprunt? Had my career come to a tragic and premature end? Don't miss next week's thrilling instalment.

For the best part of a week they balanced me and weighed me and did blood tests on me and changed the insulin types and dosages and the sheets and the pillow cases and fed me inedible food from what they called the dietetic kitchen and I fretted and became anything but calm. The first time they allowed me to get up to go to the loo I realised they were right. My legs felt as if they were trying to go in different directions. But the next time it was easier and after that I used to visit the loo frequently, not out of necessity but as a means of getting exercise and toning up the muscles. Members of the company popped in to see me occasionally and were disgustingly cheerful and told me not to worry which just made things worse and in the end I made a bargain with Dr Halliday-Croome: I'd submit to all this care and attention on one condition, that he let me out of prison in time to do the last performance of *Bunty* on the Saturday night.

He didn't like it, but eventually we agreed. They let me out on Saturday morning, still a wee bit dwaibly on the pins but feeling otherwise fine and I was tempted to head straight for the Gateway and do the matinée as well just to show them who was boss, but a bargain is a bargain and in fact I sat in the auditorium and watched the matinée and saw how good Gibbie was as Weelum. He was about forty years too old for the part, but he played it with assurance and perfect comedy timing and I couldn't fault the old so-and-so in any way. John was being careful in his movements around the stage and got up and sat down quite slowly but managed very well. Rona was still utterly beautiful as Bunty, Lennox as terrifying as she always had been in the part of Susie, Bunty's aunt, playing her with a frightening burr and calling Bunty a "nesty wassp".

I went backstage and thanked Gibbie for bailing me out and he sniffed inelegantly.

"Aye, it's a good thing Rona's keeping well," he said. "I don't think her frocks would fit me."

And I went on that night and enjoyed Weelum Sprunt for the last time, fulfilling the bargain I'd made with Dr Halliday-Croome and, I've got to admit it, feeling a lot better for my week's enforced absence.

CHAPTER THREE

Two Scrappy Seasons With A Busy Break In The Middle

So now after all these alarms and excursions we were back to normal. With John playing his original part in *Hame* I was again getting my play out which meant that after the final performance of *Bunty* I had two days complete holiday before starting rehearsals for the following play which, lo and behold, I'd already done at the Byre the previous summer. It was A B Paterson's *The Herald's Not For Sale*, only I wasn't playing the prosperous, corrupt middle-aged businessman I'd played in the original. I was playing the printer's devil in the newspaper office, Duggie Landers. Nevertheless you might well think that familiarity with the play would make it easier to rehearse and learn. Well, yes, but the fact is that for the first and only time in my life I had the script in the wings with me all through the fortnight's run for the first act. This wasn't because my memory had been damaged by recent events, it was simply because in act one Duggie had eighteen entrances, each of them with a different prop and it would have been far too easy to come on with either the wrong line or the wrong prop or possibly both. On and off I went like a demented cuckoo in a clock. The entrance was on the OP side. It's surprising how quiet the OP side of a stage usually is compared with the prompt side where the show is run from. This was no exception. The only busy person there was me. Each time I left the set there was a quick rush to the prop table and a check in the script to see where we were in the play, what to grab next and hurry back on to the stage with. No one to whisper to, no one to smile at, no one except Jimmy. Each time, there was Jimmy sitting on his stool down by the false pros giving me a thumbs up sign and a nod of encouragement and approval.

Jimmy Loughton was the theatre fireman. Every night he sat, massive and fatherly, overflowing that hard stool, watching the performance through the false pros with great interest, waiting for something to catch fire. To my knowledge it had only happened once, in the days before the Gateway Company started. There had been a production of *Macbeth*. On the first night the lights came up on the witches' cauldron scene and in Jimmy's eyes the fire under the cauldron had started to smoke in an ominous manner. It was really dry ice and the whole thing was intentional, but unfortunately no one had thought to warn Jimmy. This was his moment for saving the theatre. As the dry ice swirled thicker and thicker and the firelight flickered more brightly Jimmy grabbed the fire bucket, which probably contained more cigarette-ends than sand, strode slowly and portentously with his considerable size and weight to the centre of the stage and sprinkled some of the sand on the fire. Satisfied that he had contained a conflagration that might have destroyed the Gateway and most of the adjoining houses and shops, he turned and began to head back towards the wings but, just to be sure, half way off he stopped, looked back, thought he detected a wisp of smoke still swirling, returned, emptied the rest of the sand on the fire and finally walked off with the empty bucket. By which time the witches, non-plussed by this intruder on their blasted heath, had begun talking about their bats and newts and frogs and dogs and the stage manager had arrived on the OP side and asked Jimmy in a frantic whisper what the hell he thought he was doing, the fire was perfectly safe and he'd ruined the scene by walking on in the presence of an audience and putting the witches off their cookery. Jimmy looked suitably chastened. "Och, no one would have noticed," he said.

He was a lovely man but he reached retiring age soon afterwards and was replaced by Freddie, who was immediately christened Freddie the Fearless Fireman. Older readers will understand the allusion. Freddie the Fearless Fly was a character whose unlikely adventures were recorded weekly in either the *Dandy* or the *Beano*, I can't remember which. Our Freddie was smaller than Jimmy and wasn't as paternal a character, but he was just as kindly although he had the unfortunate habit of trying to be helpful. During blackouts Freddie would light actors and actresses on and off the set with his very powerful torch, thereby destroying the effect we were trying to create.

It must have been about this time that a significant event occurred in the Company. George took his driving test. He came in to the theatre for the performance one night brandishing the pink slip which he had earned in the course of the afternoon, as proud as punch. We congratulated him but said we didn't know he was sitting the test, didn't even know he owned a car. He said he didn't own a car at the moment but intended to rectify the omission very soon. He hadn't wanted to tempt providence either by having a car before he could drive it on his own, or by telling us what he was up to as that might have been a sure way to fail the test which, he told us proudly, he'd passed on his first attempt. A few days later he appeared with a new second-hand car and proudly showed it off to us at the top of the Montgomery Street lane. It was indeed a nice car. A Hillman

Minx, I think, but I'm no expert. There was an innocent, happy quality about its bright headlights and smooth, glowing paintwork. One careful, loving owner. It clearly had no idea what sort of life it was in for. The passing of the test was more disastrous than failure would have been because George rapidly proved himself to be the worst driver in the history of Edinburgh motoring, perhaps even further afield, and we wondered about the mental state of the examiner who had passed him. His reputation spread rapidly through the Company: if you wanted to remain alive don't allow George to drive you anywhere, even to the milk shop on the corner, and there were many excuses invented for avoiding a lift: I'd love to, but I get car sick or alternatively claustrophobic, the smell of petrol makes me ill, I enjoy fresh air, I really need exercise. George was embarrassingly generous with his offers of lifts. He offered lifts to everyone at any time of the day or night and those who weren't fast enough in inventing excuses confirmed the reputation which was already building up. While George parked the car they would appear back in the theatre ashen-faced and trembling, saying things like "Never again."

One Sunday afternoon George came out to us for a cup of tea. It gave him an excuse to drive from Craigentinny where he lived to Barnton where we lived at that time with Sheila's parents. He achieved this without any obvious head-on confrontations and all went well till after the tea party and George prepared for departure. By then it was dark. He'd parked his car only slightly askew in the driveway but, backing out on to the road, he turned the wheel too soon and caught his bumper in the iron gate. There was a squeal of protesting metal, partly from the gate and partly from the car. George stopped, got out, looked at his bumper entangled with the ironwork of the gate, surveyed the surrounding area accusingly and said, "Bad street lighting here."

It was a tough winter. There was a lot of snow which came and went, thawing and freezing. The trams up and down Leith Walk ploughed through a brown slush, sometimes soft and soggy, sometimes hard and crisp. It never seemed to get properly daylight. Looking back I'm prepared to believe now that global warming is indeed taking place.

Perhaps memory draws a veil over these few meteorologically depressing months. I can't remember the productions we did very clearly. *The Herald's Not For Sale* was followed by a double bill of Scots comedies consisting of *Rory Aforesaid* as a curtain raiser to *The Glen Is Mine*. These plays date from the 1920s and were written for the Scottish National Players by John Brandane. There must be an affinity between medicine and playwriting, because John Brandane was the pen name of Dr John MacIntyre as James Bridie was the pen name of Dr Osborne Henry Mavor. They were quite fun – the plays, I mean, not the two doctors – but unremarkable.

During rehearsals for these two period pieces we had another celebrity visit. Dame Edith Evans was appearing at the King's and Tom who, as I said, had worked with her shortly after the war, persuaded her to come down and partake of the brew of the bean of Brazil and chocky-wocky-bicky-poohs with us. She did so and I have a cutting of this episode too where we are all once again sartorially acceptable and drinking out of the same cups and saucers as last time. The caption says we were discussing the script of *The Glen Is Mine*, but I think this is a terminalogical inexactitude as the subject of the plays was hardly mentioned.

They were followed by a play by Moray McLaren called *One Traveller Returns* which was a kind of psychological drama set in a mental home. The theme was based on the quotation from *Hamlet*:

The undiscovered country from whose bourn
No traveller returns

Moray had had the basic idea for the play some time before and had apparently speculated to James Bridie about what would happen to Hamlet if he ended up in a modern mental home. Bridie had said he'd probably be looked after by a couple of psychiatrists called Rosencrantz and Guildenstern, and this play was the result of that discussion.

Moray was probably Scotland's leading man of letters at the time. He was the husband of Lennox Milne and was almost Johnstonian in his outlook and appearance. Totally impractical, Lennox said he'd been known to send for an electrician to replace a lightbulb, and she told the story of one time when she was going to be late home for lunch. She asked Moray please to remember to turn on the oven before he went out to the library otherwise, as she put it, she'd come home and find a cold fish on a dish. Walking along Princes Street at about midday Lennox's mother met Moray proceeding in the opposite direction. He raised his hat politely because he vaguely recognised the lady and she noticed, sticking in the band of the hat, a postcard on which was written in large letters, "Oven on at 12".

My diary tells me the name of the character I was playing was Dr Carnegie but whether he was a practising doctor, a clone of either Rosencrantz or Guildenstern, or an inmate of the mental home, I can't for the life of me remember. I don't suppose it matters much now.

It was only booked to run for one week, which is probably why it's not very firmly printed in my memory, and as far as most of us were concerned that was how the season petered out on 20th March 1954. Although there was one further production it was *The Heart Is Highland* which was a *tour de force* Robert Kemp had written for Lennox. This was probably one of the first one-person shows, but it was slightly different from most because Lennox played all fourteen characters. She was to revive it many times in the coming years and on one occasion, when BBC Television were doing a series of performances from various repertory companies around the country we all got in on the act and deprived Lennox of thirteen of her characters, leaving her only one. That version of the play was called *The Highlander*.

One of the main problems with The Edinburgh Gateway Company was the long summer break. Every year the season would end in March, sometimes earlier, and not resume until the Festival in August. You simply couldn't hang around waiting for the next season to start, especially when you didn't know whether you were going to be employed in it. So all of us had to look around for other work. Sheila and I had always said things would be all right so long as one of us was working but of course it would be a lot better if we both were, a philosophy which we still believe in today. So on this occasion we didn't have to worry too much, because she had auditioned for the third season at Pitlochry and had got the job so we were set up until October. The day after we finished at the Gateway we headed for London, because Pitlochry had a long rehearsal spell at the YWCA in Great Russell Street. Why they rehearsed in London at all isn't clear. It might have something to do with the fact that it was early in the year for rehearsing in a tent in the Highlands which is what the Pitlochry Theatre was. But quite a few members of the cast were based in the south in those days so maybe splitting rehearsals between London and Pitlochry kept everyone reasonably happy. Certainly Pitlochry has always had a long rehearsal period, and it was particularly so this year because the season was to consist of seven plays, five of which would be presented within a fortnight of the opening night which meant two weeks of utter chaos and every minute would be needed. We went to stay with my parents near Croydon while Sheila rehearsed and I went to many futile interviews and auditions, none of which resulted in anything.

One day while I was signing on at the Croydon Labour Exchange I met John Rae, a Scots actor whom I knew vaguely. We asked each other what we were doing in this benighted neck of the woods, and he admitted that he lived there and had I heard there was a management trying to cast four young Scots actors as the sons of Roger Livesey in a new comedy due to open in the West End soon called *Keep In A Cool Place*. He gave me the name and the telephone number and with some hope I rang them but casting had been completed the previous week. Or so they said. Maybe they just didn't like the sound of my voice. Anyway, I was too late again.

We returned to Scotland when Sheila's rehearsals were transferred to Pitlochry. These rehearsals were becoming very heavy now, trying to juggle the first five plays in the air all at once. I picked up the odd broadcast, but during this time I heard nothing from the Gateway. I'd written increasingly importunate letters, finally following Gibbie's advice on such occasions: "Get a bit of cardboard and write a stiff note", but to no avail. Then suddenly I got my first offer of a television play. It was an adaptation from the French into Scots by – guess who? – Robert Kemp of *Dr Knock, or The Triumph of Medicine* by Jules Romain.

In those days there was no television studio in Scotland, so rehearsals took place in the big radio music studio in Broadcasting House in Glasgow and we had to go to London to do the transmission. No one had even invented audio tape at that time, let alone videotape, so the only way you could transmit television was live. Once the show had started it went on till it ended or until there was some disastrous technical breakdown and the viewers had to sit and watch a screen which said "Normal service will be resumed as soon as possible," and listen to soothing music. We got close to this point several times but never quite made it. I was playing the chauffeur to the elderly Dr MacFarlane who has invited Dr Knock to take over his practice before he retires. Dr Knock was played by Moultrie R Kelsall and Dr MacFarlane by that professional road-hog George Davies. We played the first scene in the car in the studio against back projection of rolling Scottish countryside which I was told afterwards looked fairly realistic. The car was static in the studio, so there was no danger of George offering anyone a lift in it. It was the most beautiful creature and had been used as the second car in the film *Genevieve* and whenever we watch the video of *Genevieve* nowadays I lean back and say in a bored tone of voice, "Oh, yes, I've driven that one." I only had about five lines but even so it was the most terrifying experience I'd ever had in my life. I think what was really so nerve-wracking was the fact that there was absolutely no reaction to what you were doing. Up till now I'd been used to playing in theatres where you were always aware of the presence of the audience, either their laughter or even a bored cough and the rustle of a sweet paper. But at least they were *there*. Here there was nothing. Cameramen and soundmen were concentrating too much on their jobs to be interested in what you were saying. And yet you knew that out there beyond those blind expressionless lenses there was an audience far bigger than any we had ever played to in the theatre. How Moultrie got through it without drying I don't know because it seemed to me that he never stopped talking from start to finish. If this is television, I said to myself at the time, I don't think I'm in favour of it.

We transmitted it from the studios at Shepherds Bush and I stayed for the three days we were in London with my parents. My father was a general practitioner and when I got home from the transmission they were both waiting with indignant expressions.

My father was reasonably diplomatic. Nothing personal, he said, but he thought the play was rubbish. Since the theme of the play is how a crafty doctor takes advantage of gullible patients and sells them all sorts of cures they don't need, I could understand his suppressed dislike at the imputation against the medical profession. I suffered the same way from my father-in-law back in Edinburgh. He was a general practitioner as well. All I could do was shrug my shoulders.

"Don't blame me," I said, "I was only obeying orders."

Back in Scotland, while Sheila was slaving away doing performances of six different plays a week at Pitlochry – she got one of them out – I went back to St Andrews to play a part I'd played back in 1951 when the town had staged *The Masque Of St Andrews* for the Festival of Britain. It was just one of many events taking place all over the country in a fit of post-war patriotic fervour. I'd played the man in the street, Andrew Common, introducing each of five playlets set in different periods of St Andrews's history. It took place in the open air in the Cathedral grounds, a highly optimistic arrangement, but we were lucky in the weather that year: we only had to go to our alternative venue once, the Younger Hall which is big but totally unsuited for anything dramatic, having lots of steps and a startling three-second echo. This time the weather was appalling: we did one performance outside and that time the rain started half way through the second playlet and we should have adjourned or gone home. Most of the audience did anyway. Otherwise we were in the Town Hall which was pretty grotty at that time and is much smaller than the Younger Hall. But at least it didn't have steps to clamber up and down on. And anyway the patriotic fervour had disappeared in the past three years and we felt the *Masque* was something of a non-event this time round. I also did a week or so, again in the Town Hall, playing a bartender in a musical Western written by A B Paterson, called with startling originality *The West'ner*, in which I first met Una McLean whom I best remember singing her way through *Roll Along Prairie Moon* with the man who was to become her husband, Roy Boutcher.

On the Saturday night Sheila had her play off, so she caught the bus to Perth, then another bus to St Andrews to come and see me and *The West'ner*, not necessarily in that order. We spent most of the weekend sheltering from the incessant rain, and then on the Monday afternoon she started the trek back to Pitlochry. Stepping off the bus there she was greeted with the cheering news that the leading lady in that night's play, *The Master of Ballantrae*, had fallen off her bike that afternoon and concussed herself somewhat: Sheila would have to go on and read the part while an ASM took over her own tiny part of the maid. This was at six o'clock in the evening and the curtain went up at eight. The trouble is Sheila is as blind as a bat without her glasses and though she bravely managed without them for the first two acts, by act three she could no longer make out the words on the script. She had to confess failure and put them on, a pair of very twentieth century spectacles and a very large twentieth century script in a very long eighteenth century play didn't leave much room for the suspension of disbelief. I didn't see her do it because I was carolling away in the chorus of *Roll Along Prairie Moon* in the Town Hall at St Andrews, and she only did the one performance before the play came round again a week later by which time the leading lady had become unconcussed again.

You may think there was an awful lot of activity going on at this time. We were for ever flitting from town to town. Well, the fact is that that year we bought our first car. I went to Joe Munro at Kirriemuir who had an enviable reputation as a straight used car dealer. In fact he was known as Honest Joe. From him I purchased the cheapest car he had in his showroom. It was a 1935 Morris 8 Tourer and I remember its registration in a way I can't remember the registration of any subsequent car we've had. BWL 26. We called her Auntie Beenie. The name came from an occasion during *Bunty*. We had a crowd of churchgoers in the kirkyard scene and one night a friend of one of the ASMs found herself a costume and inveigled herself on to the stage unbeknown to anyone. I'd never met this person before and got quite a surprise when she walked past me, a total stranger in the kirkyard. While the action focused in another part of the forest, I whispered to George Davies who was playing Jeems the Beadle, "Who's that?" "Oh," said he casually, "it's only Auntie Beenie," and I was hysterically helpless for the next two minutes. Our Auntie Beenie was old and tired but she did her best and tried to hold herself together. She generally succeeded, apart from dropping a door in the middle of Pitlochry main street one morning and causing a certain amount of mayhem on the A9. She was noisy and draughty and she burnt oil as though there was no tomorrow, her hood frame was bent and its fabric torn and if it rained, as it did almost continually that summer, you could find your feet in puddles on the floor, but bless her threadbare tyres she lasted us a year and although she was becoming very temperamental I wept salt tears when we had to part with her for £25 to a bloke who wanted to cannibalise her for spare parts. The indignity of it – she'd cost us £120! We bought another Morris 8 from Honest Joe, a year younger and not a tourer. We called her Pandora because when we opened up her bonnet we found all the evils of the world inside. Or one of them at least: a cracked cylinder block. However, Honest Joe lived up to his name. There was no guarantee with a car of that age, but he gave us a reconditioned block for nothing, saying the car should never have been allowed out of his premises without being checked over for things like that. Pandora was more reliable and weatherproof but we never had quite the same affection for her as we had for Auntie Beenie.

During this time of much movement but little meaningful work I received a letter from Kenneth Miles saying "I think this is what you want." It contained an Esher Standard Contract. In the excitement of finally getting confirmation that I was wanted back for next season I failed to pay very much attention to the fact that the contract was only for the first play which was a repeat production of Robert's *The Other Dear Charmer*. I noticed it was being performed. under the auspices of the Edinburgh International Festival and therefore a further contract under the auspices of The Edinburgh Gateway Company would, I hoped, inevitably follow. This seemed a good enough start and I had my foot back in the door.

The trouble was *The Other Dear Charmer* meant a wig again. Now wigs and I don't agree. Let's admit it, I've got a big head. I'm not claiming that there's much in it, but it is, without any doubt, big. 7½ to be exact. The Gateway Company was lucky to have on its doorstep a first class wigmaker. A & A Wigs were – and still are – a well-established business. Adolf Theurer had founded it and now did most of the wigmaking for private clients, leaving his son George to look after the theatrical side. George Theurer used to turn pale when I walked into the shop at Canonmills. "Oh, no, not you again!" he would groan. The feeling was mutual. Nothing personal, I hasten to add. It was just that I hated having to wear his wigs, no matter how beautifully made they were and he hated having me wear them and looking a permanent mess. I very much enjoyed chatting to George. In fact, I still do because George is in the business to this day, now assisted by his own son and claiming that he's never had time to get round to thinking about retiring. But as soon as Gibbie dismissed me from rehearsal with the words, "Right, off you go to Georgie-Porgie-Wiggery-Piggery" my heart would sink. I was about to be turned into an animated haystack again. Funnily enough, a few years later George's attitude underwent a sudden change. When I walked into the shop to be fitted for a wig he didn't start to gibber and hide under the table; he greeted me calmly and cheerfully as if I were an actor with a normal head. I asked what had caused this fundamental change in attitude. "Oh, we've got plenty of 7½ wigs now," said Georgie-Porgie-Wiggery-Piggery. "We've started doing business with Scottish Opera."

But that was later. In August 1954 Georgie-Porgie-Wiggery-Piggery still had the outsize wig he'd constructed for me for the production of *The Other Dear Charmer* the previous year so it was just a question of dusting it down from where it had lain unused since I'd discarded it then. Even lovingly redressed it didn't make me look any less like an animated haystack, though.

Now, here's a warning: it's a bit about politics. Sorry to introduce such a boring and distasteful subject into something which should be reasonably pleasant and constructive but it's better to get it over with quickly. It shows a little of the murky things that were going on behind the scenes which we Thespians knew nothing about while we were innocently getting on with our ordinary jobs.

Apparently the Festival Director had made some strenuous moves to take over the Gateway for the period of the Festival. It was a first class venue and he wanted to put in an imported foreign production of his own. The Company's Council resisted this vehemently. Their argument was a perfectly reasonable one. This was the Edinburgh International Festival and if it was to be truly international there should be a contribution from the host country which there hadn't been since *The Thrie Estaits* and *The Gentle Shepherd*. The Festival Director had a different view from this patriotic one. He said he was looking at the wider picture, probably in the direction of personal kudos, and he remained unconvinced. But the Council was adamant and had the wholehearted support of George Candlish. With George, the representative of the theatre's owners, firmly on our side there was no hope of the Festival getting hold of the theatre and the idea died the death. From then on the Company presented a play as part of the official Edinburgh International Festival almost every year and the justification for doing this was shown by the fact that every year we played to capacity business and the run usually had to be extended into a fourth week after the Festival was over so that our ordinary local audience, who were so faithful to us throughout the rest of the year, could see the show at uninflated prices. In later Festival productions we had the luxury of three weeks' rehearsal because there was a little extra money available, but that wasn't necessary this year as the cast was almost exactly the same and the production more or less a repeat of what we'd done only ten months before. The only differences were that Meg Buchanan was playing the maid in place of Marjorie Dalziel, Marillyn Gray had come in to play the woman of the streets Jenny Clow which had previously been played by Kathryn Orr – and Peter Potter was producing instead of Gibbie who had got a job in London playing in the play I'd failed to talk my way into, William Templeton's *Keep In A Cool Place*.

Peter had produced the season I did at the Citizens'. In fact he had been responsible for getting me into that company. In the summer of 1952 Sheila and I had been playing a three week season with the Fraser Neal Players at the Glasgow Empress, a vast barn of a number two variety theatre later to become the Falcon Theatre and subsequently Jimmy Logan's Metropole. We had been doing three plays which were fairly sleazy in title or content or both. *Johnny Belinda* was all right in title and was a good play but it was about a rape and an illegitimate baby, not a becoming subject in the polite theatre of those days. The other two were *Pick Up Girl*, an American play about a girl forced into prostitution, and *Cosh Boy*. Peter had come to see *Cosh Boy* in which I had the rather showy part of Roy Walsh, the cosh boy who runs a gang and razor-slashes people, rapes the girls – all offstage, this was 1952, remember – and rightly Comes To A Bad End. After the second performance one night – we were playing twice nightly – I returned to our dressing room, which was about three miles up on a level with the grid, in a reasonable state of exhaustion and shortly after I'd got there there was a knock on the door and in came this hugely tall, dark-haired man with glasses. He carried a stick, and obviously had an artificial leg. "Mr Elder?" he said with the gentle politeness which always invested him. "My name's Peter Potter."

I panicked. I knew the name of course. Peter Potter was the man who had taken over Scotland's leading repertory theatre the previous year and had built it to further heights of excellence and originality. This was a bolt from the blue. I hadn't expected him. I didn't know he had an artificial leg. I offered him a chair but he wouldn't sit down. Maybe if he did he wouldn't be able to get up again. Then occurred one of the most embarrassing incidents in my life. I knew Sheila had written to him enquiring about the possibility of a job which was something I hadn't got round to yet but intended to do at the earliest possible moment. She and I were only engaged at this time but already I was making the mistake of applying a sort of proprietorial air to her professional activities and for some reason I got the idea that he was seeking my permission to interview her.

"Oh, it's Sheila you want to see," I babbled. "Hold on a minute. I'll get her for you."

And before he could disillusion me I left him in the dressing room with my colleagues who shared it with me and hurried along the corridor to Sheila's dressing room and dragged her back to ours.

That was when the embarrassment happened because he didn't want to see her at all. I'd left him alone in the dressing room with three colleagues whom he didn't want to see either. It was at this point that all became partially clear in my addled brain. If he'd wanted to see Sheila he'd have gone to her dressing room. Not mine. Our names were on the dressing room list at the stage door. He'd climbed four flights of steep stone stairs on an artificial leg *to see me!* Sheila with her usual insight quickly became aware of the situation, said something non-committal and final like, "A pleasure to have met you, goodbye," and returned to her dressing room with her dignity unimpaired by my gaffe and we were back where we started. My colleagues, taking a leaf out of Sheila's book, quickly made themselves scarce. I half wished I could do the same and go and curl into a foetal ball somewhere. But no. The great Peter Potter and I were left alone. He was charming and gracious and quickly got to the nitty-gritty, probably to prevent me from dragging anyone else out of their dressing rooms to introduce to him. He knew I'd had a long evening with two shows in a big part and I would be anxious to get back to my digs and relax. The Citizens', he said, was opening the forthcoming season with three Bridie plays as a tribute to their founder who had died the previous year. They were starting with *The Anatomist*, then they would move on to the little known *The Golden Legend of Shults* and would finish the tribute with the world première of his last play, *The Baikie Charivari* which went into rehearsal in three weeks' time. There was a small part in it which he'd like me to play and if I agreed he would keep me on for the season which ended at the beginning of June the following year. Wow! I'd never had the prospect of such a long period of work and he was offering me *eight pounds a week* – I was earning five with Fraser Neal – and if I would like to call in to the Citizens' the following morning some time before twelve o'clock when they were due to start dress rehearsing *The Anatomist*, we could finalise the arrangements. Would I like to think about it? I did. For about three seconds. The bargain was struck.

Fraser Neal was not a man who believed in contracts. I'd never had one and I don't think anyone else in that company ever had either. He was the 1950s archetype of a Scottish entrepreneur, a producer of number 2 variety shows and pantomimes and, probably foreseeing the demise of this sort of entertainment, for he was a smart cookie, he moved that year into weekly rep mode, using the theatres in which he already had considerable influence. He was the owner of William Mutrie, the theatrical costumier who clothed practically every amateur operatic company in Scotland as well as the number 2 variety shows and pantomimes, so he had free access to costumes and scenery to dress his own company, which he did. Considering the background from whence these things came it's hardly surprising that most of our productions which required clothes that were not our own had a vague whiff of Gilbert and Sullivan about them.

I did him the courtesy of giving him a fortnight's notice and I think he'd have chucked me out that night if he'd had someone else on hand to play the parts I was playing, but we parted on reasonably amicable terms. We finished that week at the Empress, moved on for a week to the Palladium Edinburgh where we subjected the local audiences to the delights of *Pick Up Girl*, then to the Palace in Dundee with the same offering and at the end of that week I said a more tearful farewell to the company and to Sheila than I had to Fraser himself. They went on to the Empire Inverness and I returned to Glasgow and began rehearsals for *The Baikie Charivari*.

I was on a high. Employment at the Citizens' was the acme of existence at that time. It should have been the happiest season of my life. But as I've already hinted it wasn't, and I have to admit that the main reason for my growing depression and loss of confidence was Peter. He was, as I've said, invariably quiet and courteous, he never to my knowledge lost his temper, but throughout the season from September till June he never once gave me a word of encouragement or advice. It was almost as though, having employed me he'd realised he'd made a big mistake and the only thing left to do was to ignore me and hope I'd go away. If he'd bawled me out and told me to act better I could have taken it and tried to do what he wanted, but there was nothing. At one point in one play, I can't remember which, I got desperate enough to say to him after the dress rehearsal when I hadn't received a single note, "Was that all right?" He considered for a moment and then said "Yes," but he said it dubiously as though he needed to consider the question very carefully and wasn't really sure of the answer.

At the end of the season it was a relief to get away. Sheila and I had got married in the April – Peter had let me off rehearsal that afternoon, but not the performance at night – and had set up house in Glasgow. Having occupied it for something less than two months we were about to leave it and never to return with any degree of permanence.

Now here was Peter Potter again. He'd done a production at Pitlochry this year so by now Sheila had finally worked with him, but with all the Pitlochry productions up and running he was free to take over as a temporary measure at the Gateway during Gibbie's absence, the length of which would depend on how long *Keep In A Cool Place* ran in London. But the fourteen months between working for him at the Citizens' and his arrival at the Gateway had been good for me. I'd recovered my confidence. I'd worked with other directors and actors and lost any sense of depression and I was determined that he wasn't going to do the same thing to me again.

I can see now that it was mostly my own fault. I'd regarded him as a god and he never set himself up as a god. I'd treated him with too much reverence and respect. I dare say he regarded me as unapproachable rather then the other way round. I should have realised that he was nothing more than a very competent producer, sometimes a brilliant one as witness his Citizens' productions of *The Taming of the Shrew* and the première of Alexander Reid's *The Warld's Wonder*. With hindsight I realise that at that time he was a man deeply troubled by what was going on inside his own psyche. Perhaps that was something to do with why he offered me the job in the first place and then, disappointed, ignored me. I have no justification for thinking this was so and never by word or deed did he give me any inkling that I might be right.

Anyway, came August and here we were home again. The Company was very similar to the previous year though Marjorie Dalziel, Ian MacNaughton and John Young had disappeared, the last only temporarily, and as yet there didn't seem to be many replacements. That was to change as we advanced into the season.

People used to ask if we found a big difference playing to a Festival audience rather than one of our own. Perhaps they were expecting us to talk about the Festival audiences' additional intelligence and sophistication. Personally I never found any difference, except the usual enormous ones that you get between audiences for the same production of the same play anyway. Certainly the Festival audiences were no better than our own, and sometimes you got the vague feeling that they weren't so good because they lacked the rapport which we built up with our own audiences, but even that isn't easy to substantiate.

But there was clearly concern amongst the Council that this had to be a roaring success. Understandable really in view of the Festival Director not wanting us and preferring something more significant and less comprehensible, so we had three dress rehearsals, followed by a photo call for the press and for our own photographer.

Stanley Ingram. He was the Company's photographer for all the time I was at the Gateway. He was gingery-haired with spectacles and many teeth and if you turned a camera on him you would need a very fast film and shutter speed because he was never still. He leapt around the stage and the auditorium, light-meter flapping, dancing frantically through the stage furnishings and shunting us around in a mad polka as he set up his shots. Very early on he earned himself the nickname of Sparking Plug. His photographs were good and clear, all black and white in those days, of course, and if he had one weakness it was when there was a stag's head on the set. Almost inevitably he would pose one of the actresses in front of it and there she would be, preserved for posterity with antlers growing out of her ears.

This year, our first in the Festival, we didn't run the extra week. We hadn't yet learnt that our own audiences would appreciate this, so we began to rehearse the next play before the Festival was a week old which made it a little difficult for us to see anything else that was happening in Edinburgh at this time.

There had come a boon and a blessing to men – and women – in the dressing rooms. During the summer some angel had rigged up a microphone over the stage with wires leading to a loudspeaker in each dressing room so that we could actually sit and listen to the performance as it took place. None of us had ever experienced anything like this before. We had never had the benefit of a call boy or call girl. Usually there wasn't an ASM available to make individual calls during the performance, and they simply came round calling the half, the quarter, the five and beginners. After that it was your own individual responsibility to get yourself on to the stage at the right time, and this was difficult when you couldn't hear from the dressing room what was going on on the stage, so the new device saved us the awful business of trying to judge when to leave the dressing room for an entrance. If you were too early it meant hanging round in the wings and getting in everyone's way and irritating the stage management, and if you were too late – well, it didn't bear thinking about. There had been some very close-run things the previous year so maybe that was why this year we had been given the comfort of the tannoy.

Our next play was *The Dashing White Sergeant* by Charles Campbell Gairdner and Rosamunde Pilcher, a new Scots comedy which had a tremendous vogue around that time. I'm not sure which company got to do the première, Perth I think. It wasn't us, anyway, though we must have been pretty close. It was done by every company in Scotland over the next two years or so, mainly because it was economically constructed with one set and only six characters. It was also a very competent romantic comedy set in an ancestral home in the Highlands with stags' heads (for Sparking Plug) and views of the loch through large windows, and was simply the story of the young daughter of the house, played by Tingle-Puss, and her wooing by two different men, hence the title. It was a sure-fire success and wasn't difficult to play and I had the nice part of the neighbouring laird who was one of the wooers, had been wounded in the war and had a gammy leg. This was slightly embarrassing with Peter producing but I managed to limp on the same leg all the time without being ostentatious about it. I got the girl in the end, you'll be glad to hear.

I got her again in the next play. Same girl, different character.

We moved from *The Dashing White Sergeant* to Bridie's last play *Meeting at Night*. Now, I've already said that Bridie's last play was *The Baikie Charivari* and that is strictly true. But when he died Bridie left another play half-finished which by now had been completed by someone called Archibald Batty and to my mind he'd done a pretty good job because you couldn't tell where Bridie ended and Batty began. It was slightly more expensive to do than *The Dashing White Sergeant* because although it too had only six characters it had two sets. We failed to grab this as a première as well, but we did get a lot of publicity about it because the Citizens' who were claiming the play as their own, which of course was their right, were opening on the same night as us so there was a big news story about the fact that the stage managers of the two theatres were in close contact by telephone – what Gibbie referred to as the far-talking machine – and that it was carefully organised that the Citizens' curtain should go up a minute before ours so that they could truly claim the première. Whether it actually happened is a moot point. I can't see it being terribly practical. There was no telephone in either prompt corner so how the stage managers were in touch I don't know. No mobiles or other modern conveniences then, of course. The nearest telephone at the Citizens' was at the stage door and the nearest one at the Gateway was in the Company Manager's office so if they'd been using those it's doubtful whether either curtain would ever have gone up at all. History doesn't relate who finished first, which might be even more interesting.

That was the end of the cosy, quiet backstage period because the next production was Robert McLellan's brilliant *The Flouers o Edinburgh*. By now the Pitlochry season was finished and many actors were free to join us for this very large-cast production. It's the only play I've ever done more than a hundred performances in. It seems to have pursued me most of my life which doesn't distress me a whit because I love it, I love the comedy, I love the language and I love all the different parts I've played in it because all five are so beautifully written. At the Gateway the stage suddenly seemed bigger and brighter and busier with all the people, the costumes and the gorgeous settings, again by Molly MacEwen. The only trouble is that each part I've played required a different wig, and over the years Georgie-Porgie-Wiggery-Piggery got a bit tired of me in *The Flouers o Edinburgh*. In this production I was playing the young clergyman who goes to London to learn to speak proper English, Sandy Lindsay, and because of the name it was felt that a sandy-coloured wig would be appropriate, so that's what I got. Unfortunately a sandy wig looks even bigger than a dark one, probably because it stands out more under the lights, and it was a correctly coloured haystack that moved around the stage in that production.

There was something funny happening about contracts. I didn't have one for the season like last year. They came along for each individual play which I thought meant they must be getting through an awful lot of Esher Standard Contract forms. In effect what it meant was that every time I had a play out now I went back to rehearsal salary of £4 10/- a week as opposed to £8 a week when I was playing. I experienced this for the first time when we'd finished the run of *The Flouers o Edinburgh*. I wasn't in the next play, *The Burning Glass* by Charles Morgan and there was a sudden drop in salary of nearly fifty per cent. What I didn't realise was that it was the first of several plays out. There were now many actors available and casting could be done much more to type than by necessity and my face didn't seem to fill many bills.

Was that the true reason? Or was there something else?

During this season I found myself much more relaxed when dealing with Peter. I was able to chat away to him, joke with him, have serious discussions with him. He hadn't changed, except that now in rehearsal he had started to give me notes and directions, not always complimentary but at least it seemed a great deal more natural. He was still thoughtful, courteous. Now he was constructive as well. It was I who had changed. I could treat him as an equal now which I hadn't been able to do before, but in spite of this more natural atmosphere, or perhaps because of it, it was fairly obvious that he thought more of some other actors in the company than he did of me. Fair enough. That's any producer's prerogative. But I use those words "thought more of" after a great deal of careful consideration and I think they're the most appropriate ones I can find though not necessarily the most natural. The comfort of it is that I don't think the words ability or efficiency came into it very much. In which case, so be it. But the nitty-gritty of it meant I wasn't high up in the pecking order for parts.

After *The Burning Glass* I was back for *The World My Parish* which was an adaptation by R J B Sellar of John Galt's *The Annals of the Parish*.

I'd met Bob Sellar before. He had done the adaptation of *The Heart of Midlothian* which had opened my first full season at the Byre in 1951 and in which I had given a dire performance as David Deans in a very short jacket and – needless to say – a very large wig. Bob was a delightful man, kind and thoughtful and at this point he was Scotland's première adapter. It was the time for many classic serials on radio and it was Bob who did most of the adaptations of Sir Walter Scott. These adaptations were long, twelve one-hour episodes as a rule. People's attention span hadn't yet been ruined by television. Bob had a tremendous facility for translating major Scottish classics into a different medium and we were to do many of his adaptations and indeed many of his original plays at the Gateway. A year later he was co-opted on to the Council where his quiet common sense was invaluable and there he remained until his death in 1960.

There was a very large cast for *The World My Parish* and I think the Council must have been getting worried about expense because for this production, and this one only, we abandoned A & A Wigs and Georgie-Porgie-Wiggery-Piggery and went to a firm in London called Bert's. The only excuse for this must have been cost: all those extra Esher Standard Contract forms, no doubt. I'd experienced Bert's at RADA because they had the advantage of being cheap but I hadn't been impressed. I don't know whether the firm still exists, probably not, and certainly if it does it won't be in the form in which it was run at that time. The wigs all gave the impression of being made of horsehair. They were as itchy as if they had been. You found yourself wondering fearfully if anyone had bothered to clean them since their last use and who had worn them then. And without the opportunity of being properly fitted you got pot-luck. There is a photograph, taken by Sparking Plug, of the cast sitting posed for a celebration of the wedding of the Rev Micah Balquhidder (Tom Fleming) and the third Mrs Balquhidder (Lennox Milne) and most of us really look like a bunch of pierrots at a beach pavilion or the inmates of a monkey house in the zoo. I am resplendent in – wait for it – a *bald* wig and it looks as if I've got varicose veins meandering across my head where the wrinkles ran. And even though there's no hair on it the wig still looks like a bald haystack if you can imagine such a thing.

We followed *The World My Parish* with Patrick Hamilton's *Rope*. Now, I don't know what went wrong here. It was a good production, the tension was beautifully built and sustained, there were a couple of frightening performances by John Unicomb, a very good Australian actor who had done the season at Pitlochry, and Tom as the two students who had done the murder, and an even more frightening one by Douglas Storm (also from Pitlochry) as Rupert, but people stayed away in droves. The reviews were bad, not so much for the production but for the play. It was dressed in the correct period of the 1920s and maybe that was a mistake. *The Boy Friend* had made the 20s a period of foolishness and fun and let's face it it's a period which makes you laugh to look at anyway. It may be that *Rope* wasn't then ready for revival in the way that Hamilton's other thriller *Gaslight* has always been. But then *Gaslight* is Victorian and perhaps that proves my point. Houses were dire. We got laughs where we didn't want them and it was depressing playing it when you could hear the echo of emptiness coming back to you from what were usually pretty full houses. Sadie had not been at work. It was withdrawn at the end of its first week. Lennox was about to go out on a Highland tour with *The Heart Is Highland* and she agreed to bring it in the following week before her tour started in order to prevent the theatre from going dark and to give the Company time to complete rehearsals of the next play, Alexander Reid's *The Lass Wi' The Muckle Mou'*.

I love this play. One of my unfulfilled ambitions had always been to play Willie Scott, the young man captured by Sir Gideon Murray who offers him the choice of being hanged or of marrying his daughter who has a big mouth and therefore no suitors. Willie takes one look at her and says he'd rather hang, but in the end common sense prevails and all ends happily. It's the classic Scots comedy, poetic in part, rumbustious in others, fast moving, full of splendid characters and language and audiences love it. But Tom got Willie Scott and I didn't get anything, which is probably just as well, because Willie was the only part I wanted to play. Tom was excellent as Willie and played beautifully with Marillyn Gray as the Lass, but that didn't make things any better for me.

After that came *Christmas In The Market Place* which again I wasn't in. Things were getting ominous.

And then came *Marigold* which I almost wasn't in either.

But before we get to *Marigold* I have a ghastly confession to make. It's another of my great embarrassments. I had written A Play. At least, I called it that. Nowadays I realise the classification is dubious. With blithe stupidity I'd set about writing the most difficult kind of dramatic piece – a farce. I called it *Outrageous Briefs* and it was the story, as far as I remember, of the marital problems of a lawyer. Hence the title, which is about the cleverest thing in it. I'd shown it to Alex Paterson at the Byre and he, being a generous and kind-hearted soul, agreed to give it a week's try-out. It was very fortunate in having Roy Boutcher and Una MacLean in it, otherwise it would have been even more dire than it was. It wasn't funny, it wasn't clever, characterisation was crass and it had no construction about it at all. I went and watched it on its first night and was thoroughly aghast at what I'd perpetrated and vowed never to write a play for the theatre again. And I haven't. It wouldn't be fair on either the actors or the audience. Thoroughly chastened I came back to the Gateway in a very subdued frame of mind. "How did it go?" asked Peter who had given me time off rehearsal to go and see it. "It didn't even start," I said.

I feel better having got that off my chest. Now let's get back to rehearsing proper plays and something really significant in the Scottish theatre.

Marigold was the New Year show as *Bunty* had been the year before. The original was written by L Allen Harker and F R Pryor, two people I'd never heard of before and haven't heard of since. It was another Scots comedy which, like *Bunty*, had done well in London, though about fifteen years later. It had Sophie Stewart in the lead. But ours was to be a different *Marigold*. Robert Kemp adapted it with lyrics and Cedric Thorpe Davie wrote the music. This was the time when the small, simple musicals were all the rage in London. *Salad Days* and *The Boy Friend* were in the middle of enormous runs, and putting on a musical version of *Marigold* was a deliberate attempt to cash in on their popularity: after all, it was the New Year show that made the money to pay for the rest of the season.

A young opera singer, Jean Carrol, played Marigold with a wicked innocence and sang the numbers divinely. There was an orchestra – well, a trio of piano, clarinet and violin – stuck in the orchestra pit which had replaced the steps and Peter was at his most imaginative and inventive. The first act is set in the village of Paradykes in East Lothian, the second in Edinburgh Castle and one of the most impressive numbers is *The Haddington Tally-ho* in which Marigold, the simple country girl, tells how she decided to travel from Paradykes to Edinburgh to see Queen Victoria's state visit. As the orchestra – sorry, trio – struck up the intro to *The Haddington Tally-Ho* there was a classical bit of stage magic.

Two of the men on stage grab parasols and open them, Marigold climbs on to a chair to sing the number, another man sits on a reversed chair and begins jerking imaginary reins and the parasols, facing the audience, begin to revolve like coach wheels. Hey presto! Two seconds and Marigold is in a coach undertaking her journey to Edinburgh and you could believe it. I used to watch that number from the wings on many nights because it was so good. There were other splendid numbers in it, rich, tuneful if slightly derivative. I remember them, as they say, as if it were yesterday. *When The Queen Comes To The North, There's A Gey Wheen Wasps Among The Rasps, What Would I No' Do For A Cuppie o' Tea* and a vigorous dance which brought the first half to a close, *The Jeely Reel*.

Sheila was in *Marigold*. She played one of Marigold's aunts, the other one being played by Edith MacArthur. Now, Sheila is very small, and Edie is very tall. Sheila played in flatties and Edie wore high heels so that together on the stage they looked like Revnell and West. To those too young to remember, Ethel Revnell and Gracie West were music hall comediennes, known as "the long and the short of it" who had a great vogue during and just after the war. Sheila wore an extremely ornate bonnet covered in feathers and fruit and, as somebody said at one point during costume fittings, everything except the kitchen sink. So she found a doll's kitchen sink and added that to the collection.

By this time we were renting a friend's flat not too far from the theatre and on Saturday the first of January we were due to do two shows. We used to say that the first show of the year – the matinée on New Year's Day – was always the worst show of the year. Mind you, the second one wasn't much better. We went in for the dreaded matinée and, Hogmanay having been fairly hectic the night before, I went home afterwards to grab an hour's sleep because I wasn't on till just before the final curtain. Marillyn, who had played the servant in the first half was at this point transformed into Queen Victoria. I announced her, she came on, stood framed in the entrance, made a few regal gestures of welcome and the curtain came down. That lasted for two performances and then the Queen's actual entrance was cut. I think it was felt that the introduction of such an important historical character so very late in the play was counter-productive. So from then on I announced her and the curtain came down before she could appear. Lese-majesty? Possibly. Anyway, that's what I meant when I said I nearly wasn't in *Marigold*. Well, I nearly wasn't in it that night because the alarm failed to go off, or perhaps I slept through it. It must have been some instinct that woke me about half an hour before I was due to go on to the stage. I rushed out to Auntie Beenie who, bless her heart, started first shot and got me to the theatre. I climbed into the clothes just in time to stagger on to the stage and announce rather breathlessly the arrival of Queen Victoria. And the curtain came down. It says something for the post-Hogmanay state of the stage management and my colleagues that no one had noticed I wasn't there and they were ploughing doggedly on through the performance, little realising that they were heading straight for a non-finish.

We had high hopes that *Marigold* might transfer to London, but it never did, though I'm still convinced that in the context of the times it would have been a huge success. A big London impresario did come to see it. He liked it but thought it was all too simple and unsophisticated and – well – *Scotch* and decided to mount his own version, new libretto – by Alan Melville, no less – new music, new cast, a chorus line, a sixteensome reel and a full orchestra. It went on with a flourish of bagpipes. I think it lasted eight performances in London.

There have been efforts to revive *Marigold* and I still think it would go well, more as a period piece than as something breaking new ground which it didn't do then and certainly wouldn't do now. But it can't be done. Like Gilbert and Sullivan's first opera, *Thespis*, the book still exists but the music has disappeared.

Many years later Sadie was trying to persuade Clive Perry to mount *Marigold* at the Lyceum as a Christmas show. Clive seemed interested. Tom had Robert's original book and lyrics, but it was at this time that Sadie discovered the lack of music. Cedric was dead. No one could find it amongst his papers. In desperation Sadie asked me if I could remember the numbers. Well, I knew the second half ones well enough because sitting getting dressed and made up while the half was playing I used to hear them night after night in the dressing room over our new tannoy. I wasn't so good on the first half though, because I didn't usually get into the theatre until the interval, but Sadie persuaded me to try to sing what I could remember on to a tape. Maybe that was a mistake. I tried but all I succeeded in doing was persuade Clive that on that evidence a revival wasn't a good idea at all. Or maybe Sadie had had second thoughts and never passed that wretched tape on to him.

I have the feeling this loss of music may not have been accidental. I don't think Cedric was particularly proud of what he had written, and it may be that after the score and the band parts were returned to him at the end of the run he destroyed them.

But that is my theory and I have no supporting evidence. There are those among us today who believe that the music may yet be lying disregarded and forgotten in some attic or cellar or at the back of a disused garage, because Cedric may simply have tossed it aside as of no importance. If so there could be a rich crock of gold waiting for some intrepid searcher and *Marigold* might yet spring afresh on to a stage to delight a new younger generation.

I hope so. Indeed I hope so. I was scarcely in it but I've spoken to many people who saw it. They all, without exception, say it was magical and couldn't it be done again?

Anyway, that was it. Thirty-three performances of one of the most charming Scottish musicals there has ever been and it disappeared into the wide blue yonder, never to be seen again.

Or did it . . .?

CHAPTER FOUR

A Short Season, A Distant Season And A Busy Season

Marigold was my last play of the season. Thanks, Peter. And thus opened what I think was the worst period of my professional life, though I know I have less to complain of on that score than many other actors. It wasn't just that there was no work, there was no prospect of work which is much worse and a deep depression was centred over the block of flats where we were living and which we still had to pay rent for with no money coming in. The supply of schools radio broadcasts which had trickled on during the previous late autumn and early winter seemed to have dried up.

There was only one gleam of light at the end of the thing that light gleams from, and that was Pitlochry. Sheila had found her season there the previous year fun and stimulating and they seemed to have been pleased with her. I had got to know the powers-that-be through visits to her the previous summer, so we hoped that there might be the chance of getting jobs there, spending the season together in a congenial setting and having a reasonably easy time once we'd got all the plays on.

A pleasant thought, and maybe from the end of January and into the beginning of February we began to build up hopes too much. Interviews for the next season were to be held in Edinburgh on 15th February and we geared ourselves up to make a really good impression at them.

Then just a week or so before they took place Sheila found she was pregnant. We were absolutely delighted, of course, but it didn't half interfere with our plans and prospects. There could be no hope for her getting into the Pitlochry company now. She'd have got away with it at the beginning of the season but by the end, in October, it would have been slightly obvious.

It added a certain piquancy to life. The old belief that we'd manage so long as one of us was working went out of the window. That idea had grown when there were just the two of us. Now there were going to be three, so it became more important that the one remaining possible wage earner began to earn wages pretty damned quick. I was well aware that it was at this stage of a theatrical couple's life that the theatre often had to take a back seat and one or other of the pair, if not both, reluctantly embraced some boring, everyday, unimaginative job with a regular pay packet and chances of promotion and improvement – doing something useful, was the usual phrase – and I was determined that that wasn't going to happen to us. By hook or by crook we'd get through this problem and come out on the other side in our right minds and doing the right thing.

Fortunately it worked. I had the interview for Pitlochry on my own and got the job, and although it was five weeks till the start of rehearsals in London at least it was something positive to look forward to and the week before they began there was a sudden rush of four schools broadcasts in three days which provided a little cash to live on during the sparse rehearsal period.

Things began to look up. Sheila got a part in the last play of the

Gateway season. It was a comedy by Bob Sellar called *Family Circle* in which she played a fourteen-year-old girl. That was asking for trouble, of course, because word had got round that she was expecting and she was immediately christened Preggie Peggy during rehearsals, or more unkindly The Tarnished Brownie.

We only had three weeks rehearsal in London before moving to Pitlochry, so we gave up the flat just before I left for the south and Sheila went to stay with her parents. Her father had been ill for some time and was getting steadily worse, and it was company and help for her mother.

I'm not going to go on about Pitlochry at any great length, just to say it was a very happy season with fewer than the usual minor irritations and the weather was unbelievably wonderful: we never experienced what all companies there dreaded – rain on the roof of the temporary building outside the inner tent which could drum so loudly it drowned the dialogue on the stage. I think through the seven months of the season we had three days of scattered showers. The previous year Sheila had had three days of sunshine. The level of Loch Faskally dropped to an all-time low and we spent hours swimming in it to escape the heat, paddling inexpertly around in boats and Auntie Beenie was replaced by Pandora.

We did six plays, not the top-heavy programme of seven that Sheila had done the previous year. They were *Dandy Dick* by Pinero, a not very funny farce about horse racing, *A Hundred Years Old* translated from the Spanish of the Quintero brothers, Shaw's *Arms and the Man* which was my play out, *The Lady from Edinburgh*, a drawing room comedy by Aimée Stewart which she'd written originally for her sister Sophie and which the bus parties adored, *The Dashing White Sergeant* again in which I played the part I'd played at the Gateway and at long last *The Lass Wi' The Muckle Mou'* in which I finally played Willie Scott. Unfortunately it was an anglicised version so that it could be understood by the tourists. It emasculated the play, and meant I couldn't get my tongue round the old Scots which I love, but it was better than nothing. Once the plays were all on we lazed our way through hot, sunny days, toured the countryside in first Auntie Beenie and then Pandora and life was good.

The sad spot was the death of Sheila's father, not at all unexpectedly, in May. He was a GP of the old school, kindly, intensely competent and caring and he had one of the wickedest senses of humour I've ever come across. He needed that to take me on as a son-in-law. The day of the funeral the producer of *The Lass*, which was the last play to go on and was still in rehearsal, insisted on keeping me working till the latest possible minute before releasing me. I prayed that Auntie Beenie, who didn't know she was under sentence, wouldn't let me down on this occasion above all others, and bless her, she didn't. I drove her as hard as I dared over the carpet of rabbits on the road – this was the year of myxomatosis – and she responded magnificently, had a short rest on the ferry, and arrived hot and steaming just in time to get me to the service.

Sheila stayed on at the Barnton house with her mother, paying frequent visits to Pitlochry during the summer and getting steadily larger, and in fact she was one of the reasons we changed cars. Poor old Auntie Beenie was sagging so much in the middle that Sheila was finding it difficult to get out of her. Pandora was younger and higher off the ground and it was possible to dismount from her with some degree of ease and dignity.

And so the season ran on through a blazing autumn and finally closed on Saturday 1st October. Our son, Simon, was born on Monday 3rd, so on paper Sheila could have done the complete season after all.

Why the name? Well, because we liked it, which is a good enough reason. But also when we got engaged we were working on *Mary Rose* at the Byre. Sheila was playing Mary Rose and I was playing the usual double of her husband and her son, Simon and Harry, so sentiment reared its ugly head too.

He was a big baby, weighing in at 8lb 4½oz, whatever that is in metric, and he looked like a baby as babies tend to do, but to us he was the most magical thing we had ever seen. He had a coating of black hair like a chimney sweep's brush, which all fell out within a day or two before he began to grow hair of the appropriate colour for his parents, a sort of insignificant mousy brown. He was disgracefully coddled by his grandmother but of course not by his parents . . . well, only very occasionally. He fed well, slept well, had an incredibly equable disposition but if he had a fault it was that he liked his meals on time. More of that in a moment.

The ending of the Pitlochry season so late meant that I missed the start of the Gateway season. Three productions had come and gone before I returned to Edinburgh. This didn't worry me too much because fortunately the broadcasts had started coming in, and for the first few weeks after I came back I was doing an average of three a week. Each of these paid what sounds nowadays like the risible sum of three pounds ten shillings except for one series which paid the much greater sum of four pounds seven shillings and sixpence because it was transmitted – live, of course, as they all were – early in the morning so rehearsals took place the previous afternoon. The worst one was a programme whose weekly transmission time was 12.40 till 1 p m, because you had to try to stop your tummy from rumbling with hunger so close to lunch. Fortunately the microphones weren't as sensitive as they are now, but there were occasions when listeners must have been irritated by inexplicable "atmospherics".

The Company asked me to do only one play in the pre-Christmas spell. This was the première (and also, I believe, the dernière) of a Scots comedy called *Our Maggy* by someone called D Heddle. D Heddle was quite clearly an ill-disguised pen name and we spent a lot of time at rehearsals trying to work out who the writer was. We tried making anagrams of the name without success – too many Ds – we looked suspiciously at the initials, but could come up with no one who matched them. You see, we didn't even know whether we were searching for a male or a female which made life doubly difficult. We thought we were on to something when we tried reversing the initials: one of the members of the Council was Henry Donald – no relation to Sheila, just another member of that prolific clan – but when we tackled him later and accused him of writing *Our Maggy* he vehemently denied it. In fact I think he took the idea as an insult. Personally, I believed him. It certainly wasn't the kind of play Henry would have penned. There were other suggestions, some of them quite intelligent, others completely bizarre and therefore probably accurate, but we never found out who D Heddle was. *At that time*, I add in italics. Forty-seven years after *Our Maggy* burst upon an unsuspecting public – in other words, just the other day – I was doing a crossword puzzle and I had to check the dictionary to see if there was such a word as hedge-creeper and there, just above the entry for "hedge" the word "heddle" jumped out and hit me between the eyes. I didn't even know the word existed. It's some technical term concerned with woollen threads in weaving. This roused my suspicions and I looked up "kemp" and found that this means the coarse rough hairs of wool. Coincidence, or have I inadvertently solved one of the darkest mysteries of the Gateway Company? Certainly we never met D Heddle. Even after the first night no one knocked on the dressing room door and said, "Hallo. My name's D Heddle. Wish I could have seen more of you." But I remember Robert Kemp came round as usual to offer congratulations.

There were new people in the Company now, already well established. Marillyn Gray of course was the most established of them all because she had appeared during the previous season and she was already famous as the deposed Queen Victoria from *Marigold* whose reign had lasted all of two performances before the costume was returned to the great wardrobe in the sky. Marillyn is one of those people so valuable in a group like The Edinburgh Gateway Company, because you can throw any kind of a part at her and she'll give it full value no matter whether it's a feeble grandmother, a girl with a big mouth, a motherly nanny or – well – Queen Victoria she'll do it with aplomb. Nowadays Marillyn is producing audio tapes and CDs for the commercial market, a technique unimaginable in the Gateway days.

There was also Mary Helen Donald – there's another of them – an elfin dark girl of huge talent who had won the Gold Medal at the Actors' Factory in its first output year. She was to stay with the Company until she got married a few years afterwards.

Norman Fraser had been in the navy for the latter part of the war and then trained at the Old Vic school in London. He still plays a mean game of golf. In his time Norman did just about everything in the Gateway except possibly cleaning out the auditorium and he'd have done that with cheerful willingness if there had been no one else left to do it. He's acted, produced, stage-managed, been Company Manager and only left when he got married to one of our passing actresses, Anne Reed, and felt he had to earn a reasonable amount of money for a man who now had responsibilities by becoming a producer at Border Television in Carlisle. What Norman doesn't know about the Gateway isn't worth knowing and in fear and trepidation I'm going to get him to read this typescript and then block my ears to stop the guffaws of disbelieving laughter which are sure to arise.

Brian Carey was a rotund Irish actor who became one of the Company's regular producers. He was cheerful, fond of the drink and therefore never very steady with his lines, and when cast in a Scots part would play it with a curious Irish accent which was never very convincing.

There was Nell Ballantyne, a lovely, elderly soul. I say elderly, but I suspect she may only have been in her fifties which is now pretty young to me. She had worked for many years in Scotland, first with the Scottish National Players and later all over the country. She had joined us for one play in the first season, *Rory Aforesaid*. Now she joined the permanent Company and stayed for five years. Nell was a delight. She was also a crossword addict like Gibbie and me. The trouble was she was never any good at them. "What's one across?" she'd ask at brew of the bean of Brazil time, exhibiting a totally blank crossword grid. We'd give her clues to the clues of increasing simplicity and eventually after a blank look which went on and on and never cleared we'd tell her the answer. She'd think about it with a puzzled expression on her face and then light would dawn and she'd tut loudly. "Och, I'd never have got *that*," she'd say. Usually Gibbie would sniff superciliously but with the very occasional clue he would nod in judicious agreement.

"Aye, it's a bit like a pail of shite from China," he'd agree.

"Pardon?"

"Far-fetched."

And there was the first of a series of three beautiful girls who came from the Edinburgh School of Speech and Drama which was what the Glover Turner-Robertson School was now called. This one was Pamela Bain who started as an ASM playing small, and sometimes not so small parts. She was bright, lively, lovely, big-hearted and very talented and her name was a gift to Gibbie. He almost immediately christened her Pea-Brain and when during rehearsal Pamela wasn't projecting enough he would shout: "Have that girl wired for sound!"

Our Maggy was set in a drama school and most of us played bright young things eagerly learning our craft from the several older members of the Company and there was a romance which built up between one of the students and her teacher. It wasn't a terribly memorable play, but it did contain one line which I've always remembered, though it wasn't one of mine. It's one of those odd quirks of memory, because it's totally irrelevant and really has no business to be lurking in my mind at all, but I pass it on merely as a curiosity. It was when the supercilious drama teacher, played by Tom, looking very seedy in a lank black wig which seemed real, damn it, spoke about the West Lothian village of Pumpherston and described how the men there "beat their wives, starve their children and feed their whippets on steak." I should ask permission to quote that but since D Heddle has never surfaced there's no one to ask, so I'm sorry, D Heddle. There's no point in revealing yourself now and demanding a fee. You've wasted enough of our time already. Come to think of it, it's a Robert Kemp-type line.

There followed three plays which I wasn't in. One was Moray McLaren's *Heather On Fire* and it was followed by Tim Watson's two plays set in Rutherglen and first performed by Molly Urquhart's Rutherglen Repertory Company, *Beneath The Wee Red Lums* and *Bachelors Are Bold*, two very funny Scots comedies which used the same set and many of the same characters. They had a tremendous vogue about that time.

Then I was back for Christmas and New Year. The Christmas production was J M Barrie's *The Boy David*, his last play but by no means his greatest, in which the boy David is a sort of Biblical recreation of Peter Pan and which contains an enormous number of additional sons of Jesse, one of whom was me. The others were played by other young actors and assorted ASMs and we had the most uncomfortable time having to cover the bare portions of our torsos with a substance which Mr Dinwoodie, the chemist on the corner of Montgomery Street and Elm Row, used to make up for us in large vats. It was called Armenian Bohl and was a sort of rusty middle-eastern colour and was very difficult to apply without ending up looking streaky. I've never heard of the stuff since and I've checked many dictionaries for the spelling but I can't find it anywhere. Bohl looks impressive though, and might conceivably be Armenian, though I'm not an expert in the language, so that's my spelling of it.

Gibbie was entering a phase of inventing theatrical riddles at this point. One of them went something like this. "Laidlaw Dalling, Lyon Todd, John Mackenzie, Liam Hood and Brian Mahoney came into the theatre to get ready for a performance of *The Boy David*. What famous Scots comedy does that remind you of?" I got it. I noticed that in the list he announced of the sons of Jesse I was the only one missing. I was also the only one of those playing the sons of Jesse who was married at that time. Therefore the others were bachelors. Therefore the answer was *Bachelors Are Bold* (Bohl-ed, get it?)

At one of the Saturday matinées there occurred a Strange Incident. Samuel (who was played by David Steuart, director of Perth Rep) and Jesse (George Davies) were discussing Biblical family matters and arguing about who begat whom, sitting upstage centre under a piece of desert canvas known to the Company as Jesse's loo, when there came a strange haunting cry from the back of the theatre. Jesse and Samuel hesitated, then continued their discussion. There came a louder cry. "Ohhhhh!" It was a sort of wail, long drawn out like a lingering cry of pain or a soul in torment. The audience stirred uneasily. Still Jesse and Samuel ploughed doggedly on. Then the door from the backstage corridor was heard to open and another cry, much louder this time, echoed through the theatre. "Ohhhhh!" Had Mrs Rochester escaped from the attic? A moment later there stepped on to the scorching, arid desert a figure in dark dirty dungarees with a dark dirty cap on top of a dark dirty face with a dark dirty sack on its back. The coalman was making a delivery. It should have arrived on the Saturday morning but he was running late with pre-Christmas orders, he was a stranger on this run and had got himself lost backstage. The three weird cries had been of "Coooal!" The coalman looked at the two strange Bedouin-like figures sitting outside Jesse's loo, his eye goggled, he spotted against the lights a sea of disembodied faces in the dark auditorium, murmured "Jesus Christ", which was a slight anachronism, and turned and stumbled off to be met by the newly arrived stage manager who conducted him safely to the boiler-room with his burden. *The Boy David* proceeded calmly and without further interruption.

Sheila had been asked to appear in the New Year play which was another Graham Moffatt comedy, *Susie Tangles the Strings*. Not so well known as *Bunty Pulls the Strings*, and not so good a play it nevertheless was seen as a good choice for a New Year audience and indeed it was, playing to virtually full houses for its allotted four weeks.

We talked about this. It raised some difficulties. Simon was still too young to be left unfed for more than a few hours, and while rehearsing during the day and playing at night was no problem, the dress rehearsal and matinée days might be. However, we decided we could cope.

The dress rehearsal was the worst. We came in as usual, but this time with a sleeping infant in a carry-cot. He was duly admired by all and sundry, which was his right and due, of course, before we deposited him with Alice Marshall in the wardrobe where he would get a certain amount of peace while Alice got on with the last minute alterations which were always necessary on a dress rehearsal day. He was sleeping peacefully and all was sweetness and light. We dressed and made up. Then there was the brew of the bean of Brazil, and we started the dress rehearsal at eleven. Dress rehearsals, especially of a multi-set production like *Susie*, tended to run a long time because the changes had to be done without benefit of Goblins. All remained quiet from upstairs. We knew it couldn't last. And it didn't. Echoing down the spiral staircase and on to the stage came the first indignant cry of hunger. It got worse. And worse. Maybe we were being over-sensitive but we didn't realise a baby could make so much of a racket. Alice Marshall coped with the rising tide of decibels, making cooing, comforting noises as though he were one of the actresses with an emotional problem, until Sheila could get off the stage and go and serve lunch upstairs, by which time we were shouting our way through the dress rehearsal. Soon afterwards all faded into silence again. We finished the dress rehearsal at a normal volume and underwent the photo call for the press and for Sparking Plug.

Matinée days were better because we deposited him, carry-cot and all, with my mother who was living nearby, and we took Pandora backwards and forwards to her flat between the matinée and the evening show. But again he was usually highly upset and telling us he was being cruelly starved by the time we got there after the matinée. Then it was the job of feeding him and, more difficult, pacifying him before we had to rush back for the half. There were a lot of matinées during *Susie*, seven altogether. Simon didn't enjoy his spell in the theatre. Maybe that accounts for the fact that he's rarely set foot inside one since.

And that was almost it as far as I was concerned for that season, apart from the last play, *Juno and the Paycock*. On 31st March we closed.

It was a good summer, though. The broadcasts came in regularly and I got two television plays. The first one was *The Glen Is Mine* which we'd done at the Gateway the previous year and in which I played the same part, and the other one was a much longer drama, adapted by Robert from his own stage play, *Henrietta MD*, which was really the story of Sophia Jex-Blake and her fight for women in medicine.

Two stage adaptations in two months might seem a bit much now, but there was nothing unusual in it then. Stage plays were virtually the only source of television drama at the time. It was to be a while yet before television really developed its own form of dramatic presentation.

The technique was still crude and unreliable. By now the BBC in Scotland had acquired an outside broadcast unit of its very own, though this was mainly for football purposes, of course, and they still didn't possess a television studio to put all the gear in for anything more important, so both these plays had to be transmitted as OBs, and the only place in Scotland with a big enough level floor space to take cameras was the Pleasance gymnasium in Edinburgh, and there they were both set up. *The Glen Is Mine* was reasonably simple and I don't remember too much about it except the normal terror of doing a live television play, but I certainly remember *Henrietta*. The first director appointed to put it on was actually a radio producer who had no experience whatsoever of television, and as rehearsals proceeded we began to get very worried about the rapidly approaching transmission day as it became clearer and clearer that the shots he was planning were totally unworkable. Fortunately the powers that be must have become aware of this situation and they managed to bring up a highly experienced director from London, Hal Burton, who arrived and took charge and very quietly but very quickly and very encouragingly turned things round. "Camera two will be here, a two shot, it'll move round you and then we'll cut to a close up on camera one and there we are – perfection." Suddenly we could see how this strange new medium should be tackled and the encouraging talk was a great help. We eventually moved into the Pleasance gymnasium where the floor was knee deep in cables, huge lights were slung from mobile gantries and all during rehearsals and transmission as well, while it got hotter and hotter under the lights, noisy kids were screaming in the park outside the windows, "We're on the telly!" There were quite a few of us from the Gateway in that production including Mary Helen Donald who played Henrietta. It was her first television performance, she was hardly ever off the screen and how she managed to get from set to set, fast, quietly, in time and without tripping over a cable I don't know.

I still didn't like television very much.

Then it was back for the Festival production which this year was *The Anatomist*. Bridie again. Tom was playing Dr Knox and I was playing his assistant, one of Bridie's thankless young men who are never off the stage and seem to be there primarily as a feed for the lead. The good thing about it was that although it's set in the early nineteenth century Lennox, who was now in charge of production, decided that I shouldn't wear a wig and all I would have to do was not have a haircut and let my sideboards grow, which I did. The result certainly looked better.

Sheila was in this too, playing the maid, Jessie Ann. The play was reasonably well received but one of the London critics laid himself open to criticism himself. Alan Dent was writing for the *News Chronicle* and he started his review by quoting the famous verse:

> Up the close and doon the stair,
> Ben the hoose wi' Burke and Hare,
> Burke's the butcher, Hare's the thief,
> Knox the boy who buys the beef.

He then went on to say, "What a pity Bridie doesn't quote this verse in his play." Well, actually he does. It starts the third act and we should know because Sheila delivered it. Clearly Mr Dent hadn't got back from the Windsor Buffet in time.

One day during rehearsal Lennox summoned me to her dressing room and announced:

"I've written a song."

I blinked in some surprise as she launched into a number to the tune of *The Finger Of Suspicion Points At You*.

> Simon's mummy's at the Gateway every other day,
> It's all because she's playing Jessie Ann.

102

Simon has to stay with granny every single day,
He does his best to be a brave wee man.
Simon's daddy's at the Gateway every single day,
It's been that way since Simon first began.
The only thing to do is be an actor too,
But what to say to Equity, to Alex McCrindle* and Equity
And Simon doesn't really think he can.

This season we acquired the second of our beautiful actresses from the Edinburgh School of Speech and Drama. Christine Turnbull. Christine came from Falkirk and she started, as most of them did, as an ASM but she couldn't be kept there for very long and was soon playing a variety of major parts. She was slim and neat and, like Sheila, as blind as a bat without her spectacles and one of the most cheerful souls I've ever met. She spent three seasons with the Gateway Company and then got married and went off to London. This was a great loss and we were all very sad, though I'm not blaming her husband, Holmes Carlile, at all because he is a thoroughly nice guy. They had three daughters and Christine unfortunately never went back into the business. That's the business's loss.

After *The Anatomist* we put on A B Paterson's well-known golf comedy, *The Open*, and followed that with a Scottish adaptation of a play originally set in the north of England called *Lucky Strike*. Conventional stuff.

Then we came to one of the strangest presentations of my years at the Gateway. This was the time when verse plays were very popular. Christopher Fry and T S Eliot were all the rage in London, and Robert Kemp obviously wanted to get in on the act. He wrote a play called *The Man Among The Roses* which was a verse play based on the ballad of *Tam Lin*. It was set in a country house in the Borders on the

---

*Equity's first Scottish Organiser

occasion of the daughter of the house's twenty-first birthday party, and alternated with fairy-like scenes in the woodlands outside. But it was the language which defeated us and I think largely defeated the audience too. It varied from the incredibly complex to the almost banal. I was playing an upper class twit at this party, all kilt and Oxford accent, and for my sins early in the first act I had to say to Gibbie who was playing the butler, "Haliburton, you seem to me a witness visibly discredited by multiplicity of twitchings." By the second week Gibbie had begun to cup his ear with his upstage hand and mutter "Pardon?" At the same time, Tom, playing the girl's father, questioning the arrival of a guest who had come in by the back door, had the immortal lines:

> But why he should disdain
> The door that's main
> Is far from plain.

Sandy McCourt who was our electrician and produced some magical effects with his lighting for *The Man Among The Roses* subtitled it *Kemping in the Blank, Blank Verse*.

The construction of the play wasn't kind to us either, because we alternated the interior set with the exterior one, but every change was done as a scene change, not as an act change so that while the stage remained quiet and untouched for the ten minutes of each of the two intervals, chaos reigned in the middle of each act. At the start of the run there were long pauses and the audience, sitting in darkness, were entertained to loud crashes and bangs from behind the curtain as the Goblins and the stage management sweated to cut down the time of the changes. Eventually Liam Hood, the stage manager, recruited all the actors in the cast into helping, and by the start of the second week we'd succeeded in getting the changes down to a quiet thirty seconds each. This was done by the actors who were

104

departing from the set after the curtain hit the deck taking specific articles of furniture and props off with them, while the Goblins flied the scenery and let in the next set, and the actors coming on to start the new scene brought on the stuff required. George Davies was playing the old minister and his job was to bring on the standard lamp after the exterior scene and set it on its mark on the stage. Unfortunately the scene change became altogether too quick for him and one night the curtain went up on the interior where George was still carefully combing the tassels on the standard lamp shade. He glared out at the audience and the saintly, white-haired old minister said loudly and indignantly, "Too damned quick!"

On the second Monday night, Tom, who had been up north for the weekend, was returning in plenty of time for the performance, but as he drove down the A9 the wind was getting stronger and stronger and by the time he reached North Queensferry the ferries had been cancelled and he had to drive round by the Kincardine Bridge. By a quarter past seven with the wind screaming round the chimney pots outside and the curtain going up at half past, panic was reigning backstage, particularly in dressing room five which I shared with the absent Tom and Brian Carey. Brian, who had been a mere Party Guest in the first act, was now deputed to go on as the father. Reading the book wasn't too bad. He could manage that all right in spite of the language. It was getting into Tom's Highland outfit which was the problem, because Brian was half Tom's height and twice his girth but we managed to get him half-pinned together to go on when the stage door clattered more loudly than usual, slammed shut and Tom came hurtling up the iron staircase, shaking – both Tom and the staircase. Tom's clothes were unceremoniously torn off a highly relieved Brian and thrown on to their rightful owner, Brian put on his own costume and returned thankfully to his own part as the Guest.

Funny play.

I don't think it would be quite accurate to say that Gibbie was frugal but he didn't seem to spend money unnecessarily and one was never aware of him either displaying great hidden riches or complaining about abject poverty. He was, I think, instinctively careful with his money, like one who has never had too much of it in his formative years. His father had been the postmaster in New Cumnock and Gibbie had helped behind the counter there in his younger days. He may have become interested in the business of banking money through his association with the Post Office Savings Bank. There was also in New Cumnock shortly after the First World War a widow woman called Mrs Telfer whose husband had been killed on the Western Front. Mrs Telfer spent many years fighting her own battle with the War Office to try to squeeze some extra money out of the Government for the loss of her prop and mainstay and by now she was becoming mentally affected by her continuing useless efforts. One day, Gibbie reports, she burst into the post office waving a Governmental letter and uttering the mournful cry, "Nae extra pension for Leezie Telfer!" This phrase with many variations became a common one at the Gateway and Leezie Telfer's name was often on everyone's lips. If you went into the Windsor on a Friday and spam fritters were off, there would be a cry of "Nae spam fritters for Leezie Telfer!" If the stage manager expected an important telephone call from a supplier and it never came through there would be an exasperated shout of "Nae telephone call for Leezie Telfer!" If the reviews in the press on a Tuesday after a first night were lukewarm, the cry would be "Nae good reviews for Leezie Telfer!" One has to assume that the Leezie Telfer story originated while Gibbie was learning about the benefits of the Savings Bank. It was about now that he started what he called "the ménage", though he pronounced it mennodj. He bought himself a pocket account book and opened a special post office account at the Elm Row Post Office, just next to Valvona and Crolla. Then he would stand outside the Company

Manager's office at midday on Friday when the ghost was walking and collar the stage manager, Liam Hood, and the ASMs as they came out with their pay packets. By fair means or foul – usually fair, one has to admit – he would deprive them of a pound from the wage packet which they hadn't even had a chance to open yet, meticulously enter the amount in his account book under the owner's name and deposit all the loot in the post office account before lunch time at the Windsor. "Better that than being peed up against a wall," he would mutter. When the ménage was a novelty there was sometimes grumbling and cursing, but when Christmas time came and money was short for buying presents Gibbie would shell out the cash on demand. There could be as much as fifteen or twenty pounds pouring into each ASM's unexpecting hands, a not inconsiderable sum in those days, and then people would bless Gibbie. After Christmas he would start again, although by now it wasn't so necessary to stand outside the Company Manager's office and rip the money off people as they came out. They came to him voluntarily, eagerly waving pound notes in his face. The benefits were now obvious and the money was willingly given. At the end of the season there would be another distribution which would help to see people through the lean months of summer. It all started with the ASMs who, as usual, were the worst paid in the Company and needed financial help, but gradually other actors and actresses asked if Gibbie would take them on as clients. The ménage became a regular institution in the Gateway Company. If anyone refused to contribute Gibbie would raise the mournful cry, "Nae money for Leezie Telfer", and he or she who refused would usually become ashamed, relent and hand over, however reluctantly, a ten shilling or a pound note. When Liam Hood married Maggie Cunningham, our scenic designer, they had a honeymoon in Yugoslavia – a rare event in those days – on their investment in the ménage.

This was all very well when the benefits of the ménage were fully understood, but in the early days when Gibbie was merely collecting money he took a lot of good-natured stick. There were loud grumblings that he was being mean and hoarding the money for his own good, that he sat in his digs in McDonald Road every evening after the show by the light of a guttering candle counting and crooning "Me gold, me gold," to himself. On one occasion these rumours were being circulated and discussed in his presence as he gathered in that week's crop of cash. Eventually he rose to his full five foot seven inches, his jaw jutted and he squared his shoulders.

"I," he announced to all within earshot, "am going to start a BEKTOG."

A puzzled silence descended.

"A what?" someone asked.

"A BEKTOG. A Be Kind To Gibbie Society. Anyone can join and there is no subscription."

And so the Be Kind Tos were born. The problem with the BEKTOG was that it could also have stood for a Be Kind To George Society and if you softened the G it sounded like Be Kind To John. There was, briefly, a BEKTOM which stood for Be Kind To Mickey – this was what Gibbie always called me – but there was confusion there too in that it might have stood for Be Kind To Tom, even though that should have been BEKTOT. It becomes too confusing to pursue further.

These next three years were my busiest. I only had one play out in each season, and once again was getting full salary even if I wasn't playing at night. The play after *The Man Among the Roses* was my play out this year. It was an Irish play called *Tolka Row* by Maura Laverty. *Juno And The Paycock* at the end of the previous season had been the first Irish play we'd attempted, but it had done well enough for the Gateway Council to widen the Company's scope. Up till now we had concentrated on English and Scottish plays, but the success of *Juno* the previous year and the success of *Tolka Row* this season obviously encouraged them to cast their net wider and what was already *the* Scottish repertory company became a good bit more international. We did several Irish plays and seemed to strike an affinity with the Irish idiom and mentality, and of course Brian Carey was keen to encourage this because it meant he got quite a few plum Irish parts. The following year we moved into Europe and tackled our first Ibsen. More of that later.

After *Tolka Row* came *Weir of Hermiston*, Bob Sellar's adaptation and completion of Stevenson's unfinished novel. Oh, dear. I don't think I was ever so miscast as young Archie Weir who rebels against his father, the hanging judge, Lord Weir, and falls in love with Christina Elliot, the sister of the Black Brothers who are border reivers. Archie is small and weak-looking externally, but strong within. I was really the exact opposite. I have never looked like a fugitive from a Gulag and by the time you've pushed me into eighteenth century costume and put another wretched wig on my head, it becomes ludicrous to think I could. However, I played the part with all the conviction I could muster, which wasn't much, and most of the reviews were kind enough to ignore me.

This was the time of the Hungarian uprising. I had an early portable radio, a big square white thing taking a huge battery which only lasted about thirty-six hours and cost a small fortune to replace. I kept it in the dressing room to get the football scores on a Saturday afternoon because I was running a pools syndicate at the time. (We hardly ever had any luck – "Nae first dividends for Leezie Telfer" – and Gibbie referred to the radio disparagingly as the "yak-box". He didn't approve of such distractions in the work of the theatre). On this we listened every night to the horrific stories of the Soviet tanks in the streets of Budapest and we heard of those who were lucky enough to get out of the country and were seeking sanctuary all over Europe. I don't know who first specifically suggested the idea, but almost spontaneously and with great eagerness we organised a midnight matinée of *Weir* in aid of the Hungarian refugees. At the time the idea took form there were only four days of the run of *Weir of Hermiston* left, so we would have to be quick to take advantage of the set and costumes still being in place. So we started. The Church of Scotland Home Board willingly allowed us to use the theatre. Bob Sellar waived royalties for the performance. Sadie's ticket printers ran off a set of special tickets free of charge and at great speed, and the seat prices printed on them were inflated as high as Kenneth Miles thought we could get away with. The usherettes agreed to work a late shift without pay. The cleaners came in to clean the auditorium between the shows, as well as do it first thing in the morning as normal. The box office ladies did their best to publicise and push the tickets to anyone who came in. Sadie made telephone calls to her Women's Rural Institute secretaries and threatened and cajoled. It was astonishing how everyone was keen to help, from the Goblins, who stayed on to run the show without pay to Mrs Tait and Margaret and the middle-aged ladies in the tea-room who bullied the baker to supply an extra batch of scones and cakes for nothing. When the baker knew what it was for there wasn't much bullying needed. Kenneth Miles organised an auction in the tea-room during the intervals and every local shopkeeper presented us with items to be sold there. The Muirs contributed a case of whisky. We asked the Lord and Lady Provost to attend and they agreed without hesitation, even postponing a previous engagement to do so. The BBC mentioned it on radio and television, and the press covered the event with several stories. The publicity was enormous, and it had to be for such a hastily organised event.

It's difficult now to understand the horror and revulsion that swept the country at the time of this act of barbarism, the helplessness and uselessness we all felt in the face of monstrous aggression, and I think the huge outpouring of generosity, not just in the small sphere of the Gateway Company, but throughout the United Kingdom with many similar money-raising events, helped to salve our consciences to some extent.

Maggie Cunningham and her staff in the scene store made hand-painted placards advertising the performance. We tied them all over Pandora and drove up and down the streets of the city centre in her advertising our wares. Someone lent us a loudspeaker and a microphone and Norman Fraser trumpeted the news all over town. There were no traffic lights on Princes Street then, just a series of policemen on point duty, two of them at the West End, two at the Mound and one at each of the junctions, and as we drove along Princes Street towards the Post Office and Register House, heading for Leith Street and back to the theatre, one of the two policemen on point duty there spotted this incredibly untidy car approaching him with the loudspeaker blaring. A majestic white-brassarded arm went up and the traffic in all directions ground to a halt while he advanced towards us with the measured tread usually reserved for monarchs and archbishops at coronations. He stopped at the driver's door.

I lowered the window and said brightly:

"Good morning."

"What's all this then?" he asked.

I thought of telling him it was a car and we were in it but didn't think that would be wise.

"We're doing a midnight matinée tomorrow night," I explained. "For the Hungarian refugees."

"You're not allowed to advertise on Princes Street," he said.

It was the first opposition we'd struck and it put my hackles up, but carefully.

"It's all right," I said. "The Chief Constable knows all about it. Doesn't he, Norman?"

Norman backed me up like a trooper.

"Oh, yes, Willie Merrilees," he said, name-dropping like mad and with that wide-eyed innocence he's so good at. "In fact I think he's coming to the show, isn't he?"

"You know, I think you're right," I said, and we held our breaths. We knew no such thing, of course, but the traffic was building up in all directions, our *eminence grise's* colleague was wondering what to do with his share of it and the odd car horn was beginning to sound impatiently.

It took the wind out of P C Plod's sails, anyway. He looked as nonplussed as his bap-like face could look. "I have not been informed," he said. We shrugged our shoulders sympathetically. Really, the inefficiency of these chief inspectors! "Aye. Well. Get on. You're holding up the traffic."

So we got on and he went back to sorting out his self-inflicted chaos. In mitigation of this petty bureaucracy I have to admit he probably had his own problems. The trams had recently been withdrawn and he was only just getting used to the directions the buses were going.

It was a remarkable night, that Friday. It had been organised and publicised in the space of three days, the house was full at grossly inflated prices. I'm told the Chief Constable was actually there. We presented the Lady Provost with a bouquet of flowers which had been donated by Rankins, the fruiterers at the corner of London Road and she handed it to Kenneth Miles for his auction. It was bought by one of the audience who immediately put it back to be auctioned again. It was bought again and put back again. By now the flowers were beginning to look a little dizzy and confused, but it didn't matter. In the shadow of those Soviet tanks we all experienced the warmth of genuine human care and concern.

The curtain finally came down at about half past two in the morning. We'd done two shows virtually one after the other. Each of the two intervals had been extended to about half an hour to allow for the auction. The next day was Saturday and we had a rehearsal in the morning followed by two more performances. Then there was a change-over weekend and on the Monday we opened the next play,

Johnnie Jouk the Gibbet. But we all felt it had been worth it, and I believe the final total raised came to over a thousand pounds. What's that equivalent to in today's money?

Johnnie Jouk the Gibbet was another Scots comedy by Tim Watson. This one was set in the seventeenth century and concerned the problems of the Glasgow Town Council at the time, always a ready subject for mirth in Glasgow and even more so in Edinburgh. Johnnie McLellan, a ne'er-do-weel, was caught by the council for many misdeeds and imprisoned to await hanging, but they found they hadn't got a hangman, and eventually by complex means ended up employing Johnnie to do the job himself. All good fun. I played the Provost. I had a wig. But this one was fine, because Lennox felt I should be a Falstaffian Provost, so I ended up not only with a bushy grey wig, but a bushy grey beard, a bushy grey moustache, bushy grey eyebrows, padding all round me, and even padded tights. One of the reviews complained that I was a bit stiff, which is fair enough. I was. I could scarcely move in that lot and was it hot! After the dress rehearsal was over we had notes and while we were getting them I absent-mindedly peeled off the eyebrows, the moustache and the beard because I find them intensely itchy and uncomfortable and can't wait to get out of them at the best of times. When the notes were over I headed happily for the spiral staircase and was half way up it when I was hastily summoned back to the stage. In the desire to get rid of the discomfort I'd totally forgotten about the press call and Sparking Plug. No time to stick the damned things on again with spirit gum, so I managed to press them all back on in a temporary sort of way and returned to the stage for the photographs. Looking at them now I'm well aware that the old face looks stiff as I try to keep all that extraneous hair in place. It's hanging there by a thread. During one of the performances the left eyebrow worked loose and I played almost the whole act with the thing hanging down over my eye and terrified that it would drop off completely so that when the curtain finally came down I was cross-eyed and feeling like Admiral Nelson.

At one point the Provost has to order his serving maid Morag to bring him a rope so that he could threaten to hang Johnnie. Now we weren't quite sure how to pronounce the word and Gibbie, who was playing the Town Clerk and whose command of old Scots was encyclopaedic and authentic, was at his most gnomish and said that it could be pronounced either rope or rape and he would follow whatever I said because I was the first one who had to use the word. I knew Duncan Macrae had played this part not long ago, so I asked Gibbie:

"How did John pronounce it?"

"He pronounced it rape," he said.

"Right. That's what we'll call it then," I said, a man of instant decision.

But I'd reckoned without Mary Helen who was playing Morag. I had to shout offstage to her:

"Morag – fetch a rape!"

"A *whit*?" she asked. By the second week she was saying it in a tone of astonishment and outrage. I had to say it again.

"A rape," I said.

"Rape?" she asked slowly and carefully, as though savouring the word.

And looking offstage I could see her standing there with a look of wide-eyed innocence on her face and most of the stage management splitting themselves with silent laughter.

I wished we'd decided on rope.

Another Gibbie pronunciation story. He told us that words like something, anything, everything in old Scots should never drop the final "g". "You don't talk about a 'thin'," he'd say. "You talk about a 'thing'. So it's some *thing*, ony *thing*, aa *thing*." We duly took this in, but sometimes "naethin'" would inadvertently be heard. "Ni *thing*. Ni *thing*," would croak that familiar voice. "Nathan was a prophet."

Johnnie was followed by the première of *The Wax Doll* by Alexander Reid. This was an unusual play for Alex, unlike his Scots costume comedies which had large casts and several sets. *The Wax Doll* had a cast of six, one set and was a serious modern play concerned with faith healing, which was a subject dear to Alex's heart. It was almost brilliant but just missed in spite of a great performance by Mary Helen as the crippled girl confined to a wheelchair and a brilliant one by Roddy MacMillan as Sardou, the music hall entertainer-cum-faith healer who doesn't understand his own powers. Perhaps people were expecting more of the Alex Reid they knew of old. I don't think the play has been seen since, which is a pity.

And then it was Christmas and New Year time again and we did our third and final Graham Moffat, *A Scrape o' the Pen*, which ran for five weeks to packed houses, but wasn't as good a play as either *Bunty* or *Susie* and became rather tiresome towards the end of the run. Odd little bits of extra unrehearsed business appeared and Gibbie would slap some wrists when he saw the introduction of these.

"Sorry, Gibbie," we'd say. "It just crept in."

"Well, it can just creep out again," he would say emphatically.

About half way through the run George began to get restless. Jenny, his wife, was due to go into hospital for some minor operation. George became more like a cat on hot bricks as the day approached. He spoke to us all about it. All the time. We made encouraging noises and told him not to worry. He agreed not to, there was nothing to worry about, it was a perfectly simple minor operation, people had them every day, and he went on worrying worse than before. He'd got everything organised. She would only be in for three days maximum and George would be looked after by his daughter Joan. He'd made complicated arrangements for Jenny's convalescence when she came out. The night before the operation we wished Jenny good luck through George and went about our business till the next performance because we hadn't yet started rehearsals for the following play.

The next night we were sitting in dressing room five making up when there was a tap at the door and George poked his head round. One look told us the story. No one said anything for a while but I think eventually it was Norman who had the courage to ask how Jenny was.

"She died under the anaesthetic," said George simply.

We made all the appropriate noises which seemed totally inadequate in the circumstances as we looked at the drawn, lost face in front of us. After a minute George smiled a strained smile, withdrew and we heard him going into dressing room six next door and the cheerful murmur of conversation which we'd heard through the wall died and there was silence.

That night George went on and gave probably the funniest performance he had given in the part he was playing. We listened over the tannoy to the projection, the timing, the gales of laughter from the unconscious audience, and we wondered at the sheer courage of the man. Long afterwards, when he could talk about it dispassionately, George said it wasn't courage. Simply going on that night saved his sanity. But there was a lot of courage there as well.

The next play was another Moray McLaren, *Muckle Ado*, which was a comprehensive send-up of Scottish Nationalism, London Government, the Kirk in Scotland, the BBC, the press, the American way of life and almost everything else you could think of. In fact there was almost too much. The whole plot was set off by the discovery in a cave in a Perthshire hillside of something that could be the Stone of Destiny. Civil servants got shut into chests, there were chases and fights and it was all frenetically active. It was also another occasion like *Meeting At Night* when the Citizens' were mounting the play on the same night as us, only this time, because Moray was virtually a part of the Gateway, we were claiming the première by taking the curtain up a minute before the Citizens'. Frankly I think this publicity story was wearing a bit thin and I still have doubts about how authentically the whole thing was organised. I played the minister of the local village, probably the only really sane character in the play. He was an elderly gentleman, this minister, and there was general agreement that I shouldn't be provided with a wig, a decision I approved of wholeheartedly. But I would have to grey my hair. Norman, with whom I was sharing dressing room five, said that he'd achieved impressive results in his student days by the use of a tube of Meltonian white shoe cream, the stuff you used to whiten canvas gym shoes. So I tried it. It certainly whitened the hair but left it looking strangely stiff and spiky. It also meant for the first time in my life I became the possessor of A Hat. This was necessary, because the Meltonian shoe cream had to be applied before each performance and washed out afterwards, but on Saturdays I simply refused to wash it out between the shows. Too much like hard work. At this time I was walking from the theatre after the matinée to my mother's flat for tea, and then back to the theatre for the evening show, and I couldn't be seen with my stiff white spiky hair in the street. It might have caused heart attacks or ribald comments. So I bought a hat. Size 7½. It was a brown trilby-like thing, very smart and, worn at a sinister angle, I thought it made me look very like Humphrey Bogart. No one else did, however, and after the run of *Muckle Ado* the hat hung for years gathering dust on a peg before finally being thrown out in a particularly violent spring clean. I've never worn any kind of headgear since.

The Company split in two after *Muckle Ado*. There had been an agreement of some kind with the Arts Council that they would give us a bigger grant if we were to undertake a winter tour playing one night stands for a fortnight round the Borders. I don't know how much the additional grant was, but it must have been substantial.

Apart from the cost of mounting such a tour, it meant hiring almost double the number of actors in order to keep two companies going at the same time.

I never went on a Gateway tour. I was always kept back with the home company and was secretly quite glad of it. While the hey-for-the-open-road, roving-gypsy life sounded romantic and exciting I doubted whether it would live up to expectations in the normal Scottish Borders winter, and when the touring company came back with horrific tales of digging the bus out of snowdrifts and being lost in a blizzard on the Grey Mare's Tail, I realised that home comforts had a lot to recommend them.

Unaware of the dangers they were facing the tour company happily rehearsed *A Nest of Singing Birds*, a Robert Kemp play originally entitled *The Scientific Singers*, which had to do with the difference between plain singing and part singing in church which doesn't sound madly hilarious, though I believe it was. I never saw the play, even though it had been done at the Gateway in our third season, but that was during the Peter Potter regime and was one of the many plays I wasn't in. The tour company mounted their bus and went roaring off for a fortnight's stay in points south while the home company did two premières during the time they were away. Having just done a play based on a possible Stone of Destiny the next one was *The Tinkers of the World*, by Ian R Hamilton who was best known for having himself recently helped to steal the real Stone of Destiny from Westminster Abbey. Or was it the real one? Let's not go into that or we'll be here till Christmas. The play concerned the depopulation of a Highland island, inhabited by the same family for hundreds of years, now facing a compulsory purchase order so that the Government could turn it into a rocket range. It won an award for the best new play in Britain in 1957 and I can't remember much more about it except that there was a lot of talk and not much action. The second play was by Albert Mackie. It was called *MacHattie's Hotel* and all I can remember about this one is that it was set in a small hotel in Edinburgh's New Town and I played some kind of plain clothes policeman who spent most of his time talking about the evils of international communism, a subject much on people's minds at that time after the Hungarian uprising.

During *MacHattie* the touring company returned and we began to rehearse together again, while at the end of *MacHattie* those who had helped to augment the home Company left us and we contracted to normal size. We went back to Barrie, and did *The Admirable Crichton* which many of our audience insisted on calling the Admiral Crichton as though it were a pub. After that we did *The Playboy of the Western World* as the last play of the season, the classic Irish play by J M Synge which we did rather well, I think. I can say that because I was barely in it and could afford to sit back to some extent and watch it dispassionately. Norman played Christy Mahon and George Davies made a vicious old man of his father and the company closed down on 30th March for the summer.

CHAPTER FIVE

Two Crowded Years With A Sudden End

In the middle of April Sheila and I went on our honeymoon. It was only a little over four years late. We left Simon for a week with his maternal grandmother and we boarded the *St Ninian* at Leith Docks on the Monday and sailed for Aberdeen, then on to Kirkwall, north to Lerwick, back to Kirkwall, then to Aberdeen again and so back to Leith by the Saturday. The *St Ninian* was the flagship of The North of Scotland, Orkney and Shetland Shipping Company and she was very comfortable. It was a wonderful trip, in spite of a Force 10 gale between Lerwick and Kirkwall, and it's a pity the chance of doing it no longer exists. During that time I experienced the most incredible piece of luck. A few weeks before we were due to go I was rung up by a producer at the BBC in Glasgow, Roderick McLean, and asked if I could read a Morning Story live on the radio on the Tuesday morning of the very week we were away. In Glasgow. It was like drawing teeth. Morning Story was highly prestigious and I hadn't done one before, but I said I couldn't do it as we'd be on our delayed honeymoon.

"Oh, where are you going?" asked Roddy, because he was a nice man and interested in that sort of thing. I told him. There was a pause at the end of the line. "Now listen," he said. "What time do you dock in Aberdeen on the Tuesday morning?" I said I thought it was before dawn. "And when do you sail?"

"Two o'clock," I said.

He thought for a minute, then said: "I've got to go to Aberdeen some time that week anyway. Suppose we transmit it from Aberdeen? We'd rehearse from ten till eleven at Beechgrove Terrace, transmit from eleven to eleven fifteen and you'd be back on the boat for lunch."

And that's what we did. Talk about combining business with pleasure! Though it didn't leave us much time to explore Aberdeen.

A week later I was in London for the Equity annual general meeting. I'd taken on the job of Equity Deputy – what Gibbie described as the Equity Nark – for the Company the year after it started when Ian MacNaughton, who had been the first Nark, left. I did this not through any great trade union belief, but because somebody had to do it and you got a small fee for everyone you enrolled as a member. It also meant you got your fare paid to the AGM, so I made the most of it and spent a lot of time seeing shows and people I hadn't seen since I left RADA.

I did a show at Perth Rep, the first time I'd ever played there, and then there was enough sporadic broadcasting throughout the summer to keep us going till the season restarted.

This time the Festival show was a revival of *The Flouers o Edinburgh*. I was playing a different part in a different wig and I think as we began working with increasing intensity at rehearsal we all realised that we had something rather special here. It was going to be an altogether better presentation than our previous one. Duncan Macrae had been offered a part in it, any part he liked, if he'd just lend his name to the production. Lennox told me later she was astonished when he chose the small part of the Nabob who appears in the second act and then never appears again. But, she said, she realised after the show had been running for a week how wise he was. It was a spectacularly showy part, it was pivotal to the plot, he didn't have to come into the theatre until act one beginners were called and he could spend the third act with his feet up in the dressing room waiting for the curtain call.

But the star of the show was Walter Carr as Jock, the servant. With a succession of trays of tea and scones he shambled round the stage, turning corners without a bone in his body, a high white hat like a chef's bobbing up and down, modelled on Alan Ramsay's hat on his Princes Street statue, and working without his teeth which was good for a dozen laughs before he started, it was a classic comedy performance immortalised in Ronald Searle's cartoon in *Punch*.

Pamela appeared in the wings at the dress rehearsal looking utterly fabulous in a hooped gown with a very low décolletage. Brian Mahoney, who was now our stage manager, allowed his glance to sweep across her, did a double-take, returned and stared at the impressive frontage.

"Are those safe?" he asked incredulously.

"Oh, God, I hope so," was Pamela's heartfelt reply.

The play created quite a sensation amongst the London critics who had never seen it before, of course. W A Darlington, the drama critic of *The Daily Telegraph*, collared Gibbie in the Windsor Buffet after the show and went on and on about the fact that he had never considered the difficulties of the English language for the Scots after the Union when all Scots were desperate to learn how to speak what was then considered to be proper English. He thought the play deserved a run in London.

It was a big cast and the dressing rooms were very full backstage. This season we welcomed the third of our beautiful girls, Evelyn Elliot who stayed with the Company for three years and excelled in cool, calculating parts, the upper-class aristocrat with a smell under her nose who had just tethered her horse at the stage door, which was actually totally against her nature. There also joined us a young man from the Actors' Factory who started as an ASM and later played leading parts before going on to become an announcer with Scottish Television and later to gain fame as Dr Finlay with Andrew Cruikshank and Barbara Mullen – Bill Simpson. While *The Flouers o Edinburgh* ran through the Festival and for a week afterwards we were already rehearsing the next offering which was Bridie's *Dr Angelus*, for which Duncan Macrae was staying to play Angelus.

I'd met John Macrae three or four years before at the Citizens' and knew him quite well as the Chairman of the recently formed Scottish Committee of Equity where his methods of controlling meetings were, shall we say, unconventional. During one Scottish annual general meeting while a debate on the plight of the number 2 variety theatre chorus girls was becoming dangerously heated, he suddenly slapped the table and said, "Did you hear about the man in the cocktail bar of the *Titanic*? He said, 'I asked for ice in my whisky but this is ridiculous.'" The meeting dissolved in laughter, the tension was broken and we were able to return to a more constructive debate. Many people found him either tiresome or eccentric, sometimes both. ("Macrae?" said Gibbie. "He couldna time an egg.") Eccentric he may have been. And his stage discipline sometimes left something to be desired. ("You stay right downstage there, darling. I'll be up here picking flowers.") How could anyone with a face like his not be eccentric? But if ever a face was a fortune his was it. And personally I found him one of the kindest men I've ever met. When a few years later Sheila and the family all got sick with different things over Christmas, John was starring in a show I was doing in Glasgow. It wasn't very successful and he had problems of his own trying to make it work, while I was at my wits' end not knowing what disaster I was going to find when I got home, but John was the only member of the company who asked after them every single day. I've never forgotten him for that. I got to know him well during *Angelus* because I was playing Johnson, another of Bridie's thankless young feeds. We were on the stage together most of the time and being a fitness freak he dragged me for a brisk walk round Calton Hill between the matinée and the evening show on the Saturdays during which he expounded his complex theories on life, the profession and the universe, not one word of which I understood.

The day after we opened we started rehearsing the next play which was a strange Irish piece by Lennox Robinson called *Drama At Inish*, and John went back to the Citizens' to start rehearsing *Twelfth Night* in which he was playing Malvolio. Evelyn was playing Mrs Corcoran in *Angelus*, and we had a scene together in the first act when Angelus wasn't on. Unfortunately John was in his dressing room and a great deal less than a thousand miles away, and he started to go over Malvolio's lines to himself. Loudly. The voice reverberated through the closed door between the backstage corridor and the stage, and there was no doubting John's ability to project.

"M – O – A – I – doth sway my life . . ." came booming round the stage and out into the auditorium.

Someone will tell him, I thought to myself optimistically. It'll only happen the once.

But next night it happened again, and Evelyn and I found ourselves shouting at each other, trying to overtop the sound of Malvolio so that it didn't reach the audience. We failed. When the curtain came down at the end of the act I walked off the stage into the wings and found Brian Mahoney.

"Could you ask him to shut up?" I asked.

"How can I shut him up?" Brian objected. "You're talking about Duncan Macrae. Why don't you do it?"

"Why me? It's your job."

"Yes, but you're the one that's suffering."

I felt like saying that Evelyn was suffering too, but it didn't seem fair to ask her to go and tell John to keep quiet. So I took a deep breath and went to his dressing room – he was in number two downstairs – and explained our problem as tactfully as I could and said it was a little disturbing and could he at least keep the door shut? He was utterly devastated that he should have been causing disruption on the stage. I believe he went to Evelyn and apologised to her as well, and from then on Malvolio must have been gone over *sotto voce* or not at all, because we never heard another word.

Towards the end of the play, Angelus knocks Johnson unconscious, stretches him out on the examination couch and then has a long speech explaining his ethics over the unconscious body. There's a ring at the front door bell. Angelus runs off and a police inspector arrives as Johnson recovers consciousness, the inspector has a short scene with Johnson in which he has one of Bridie's best lines, "You did your best and it wasn't very good, and that's a fair enough epitaph for most of us." Then Angelus is led back on in handcuffs by a policeman before being taken away. The first night of the second week this all happened as usual, but when John was brought back on in handcuffs I found my eyes riveted on his face. He looked as white as a sheet. Had he fallen over in the wings and broken an ankle or a wrist or something? The curtain came down, John made yet another of his embarrassing curtain speeches, and when the curtain finally fell I asked him if he was all right. He seemed puzzled, so I explained that he didn't look well. Light dawned on the lantern face. Yes, he was fine, but he'd discovered that if he removed his make-up during that brief spell offstage he could just catch the ten o'clock train home to Glasgow.

I mentioned his curtain speeches. They were famous. One night in *Angelus* he told the audience he wasn't terribly keen on Saturday night audiences because they were too much inclined towards frivolity. That was on a Saturday night. A couple of other classic stories. Coincidentally, the day Bernard Shaw died John was appearing in a Shaw play at the Citizens', and in his speech at the end he announced the passing of the playwright. "This is a dead loss to the theatre," he added. On another occasion during the Henry Sherek season at the Lyceum, he was doing a Biblical play called *Judas Arise*. Yvonne Mitchell had co-starred with him in it, playing Mary Magdalene. "I have to thank Yvonne Mitchell for coming and playing the whore. I can think of no one more suited to the part."

Embarrassment over and back to the plot.

Drama At Inish was followed by three premières in succession. First came Moray McLaren's *The Non-Resident* which is an example of the problems arising when a playwright writes a part for his wife which he believes to be right up her street but which in fact she isn't really suited for. Lennox was asked to play a vibrant, passionate, sexy woman who took a young lover, played by Bill Simpson, and it simply didn't come off. I think Lennox felt this deeply herself because she never seemed happy in the part and couldn't have been more relieved when the run was over.

It was superseded by Robert Kemp's *The Penny Wedding*, another backstairs Scots comedy which was quite funny and easier to understand than *The Man Among The Roses* and gave scope for several over-the-top performances but is mainly memorable for being the play in which Gibbie dried. This was an event unheard of in the annals of the Scottish theatre, and when Gibbie dried he did so monumentally. The problem was that he was now too deaf to hear a prompt, and although the ASM tried to give him the line Gibbie simply couldn't pick it up. Everyone else in the theatre could. Gibbie looked round, saw everyone gazing at him expectantly and he turned to Bill Simpson who was standing next to him on the stage.

"Is it my turn now?" he asked.

Bill nodded vigorously.

"What do I say?" asked Gibbie.

Bill, who had picked up the prompt from the ASM, told him. Loudly. There was no point in trying to be subtle about it.

"Oh, aye," said Gibbie in a tone of happy recognition, and went blithely on with the line.

It was all done so easily and relaxedly that I don't think many people in the audience fully realised that anything had gone wrong.

There was romance brewing backstage. There had always been romance, but this one you couldn't ignore. Pamela had discovered Bill and Bill had discovered Pamela. You used to bump into them in tight clinches in odd corners all over the theatre. One night during a performance Gibbie came into the wings to make an entrance and, in the light-spill from the backstage corridor door, he spotted Bill and Pea-Brain standing where they thought they couldn't be seen lit up for a split second with their arms tight around each other. Gibbie snorted loudly and said in ringing tones:

"I've seen a pair of dogs getting a pail of water thrown over them for less."

After *The Penny Wedding* came Bob Sellar's *Arise, Sir Hector*, the story of a man achieving a knighthood through dubious means. My main memory of this play was that near the beginning Tom had to punch me on the nose. We spent quite a lot of time working out how to do it and eventually found a pretty efficient method of making it look good. Tom would wield a fake punch. He hoped it would look like a real punch and I hoped it wasn't. I had in the breast pocket of my jacket a handkerchief in which I had smeared a generous blob of Gordon Moore's toothpaste. I don't think they make Gordon Moore's toothpaste any longer, but it used to come in a maroon-coloured tube and was blood red when you squeezed it out. It was supposed to impart a healthy tinge to your gums or something. Anyway, I turned the hankie over to hide the toothpaste and pushed it carefully into the breast pocket. After being hit I emitted a loud cry of pain, pulled the hankie out of my pocket, held it to my nose, opening it out as I did so to smear the offended conk with the hidden Gordon Moore's toothpaste and then exposed it to the public gaze. It was amazing the amount of whispering that went on in the audience. I don't think they were saying, "Oh, poor fellow, look at his bleeding nose!" They were just saying, "How on earth did they do *that*?"

We had a really good romp after that. J B Priestley's *When We Are Married* in which I played the photographer, drunk throughout the performance, and Sheila, who hadn't been with the Company since playing Mrs Angelus and being murdered nightly by John Macrae returned none the worse to play a ferocious Mrs Soppitt.

Then we went international. Ibsen's *The Wild Duck* which I think we did pretty well. It wasn't exactly a bundle of laughs and the houses dropped off a little, but that was to be expected and those who came seemed to enjoy it.

We should know. By now we got told direct. We'd had inflicted on us the ghastly business of meeting the audience after the first night. Eager customers would gather for yet more of Mrs Tait's tea and scones and we would clean off the make-up and get changed into our normal clothes and creep like snails unwillingly to the tea-room to make polite conversation and be charming and listen to what the audience had to say. We felt it was a little hard on us, seeing that we'd had a long day with a dress rehearsal followed by notes followed by a press call followed by Sparking Plug followed by a first night and we were facing a read-through of the next play at ten o'clock in the morning, but I think the management were becoming seriously worried about the effect of television on audiences and there were certainly signs that things weren't quite so good as they had been. We had already started offering two seats for the price of one on first nights, thereby drawing more people early in the run and so spreading the word round the city quicker than might otherwise happen. This was another way of supporting the same idea. It went against all our instincts. Nowadays it's perfectly natural to appear out front after a show to partake of a reviving drink or meet friends. Then the strict rule was that you were *never* seen by the audience after a show unless they came backstage to see you. So this was a deep and unpleasant culture shock and we found it frustrating listening to eager middle-aged ladies saying things like, "Don't you ever get your parts mixed up?" In answer to which we felt like saying, "I think, madam, that would be anatomically impossible." And then of course there was the classic unconscious insult, "What do you do during the day?"

"We work, madam."

"Oh, I'm sure you must do. But what at?"

"We rehearse, madam. We learn lines, madam. We sweat our guts out, madam, to prepare a play once a fortnight for your entertainment and diversion, madam."

"Oh . . . I see . . ."

"No, you don't, madam. You don't see at all. And why should you, madam? Your job is not to understand how it's done. Your job is to sit back and enjoy. It's our job to present a smooth, finished article to you where you can't see the joins of hard work. But I do wish you had the insight to understand, madam, that we don't wave a magic wand and it all just happens."

This is not to be taken as an example of the kind of conversation we actually had in the tea-room, more as an example of what we would like to say after a long hard day, only perhaps not quite so politely.

I played Hjalmar Ekdal in *The Wild Duck* and Gibbie played Old Ekdal, my dear old father. At one point in the second act I had to help him out of his chair in which he was dozing rather noisily and conduct him off the stage to bed. By the second week, as we went towards the exit Gibbie, apparently half asleep, would mutter to himself in that voice which could be heard at the back of the auditorium:

"Toofie-pegs . . . *Pee-pees* . . . Bye-byes."

It was all right for him. He could return to the dressing room, satisfied with a job well done. Well – done, anyway, but I had to go straight back on again and try to keep a straight face.

One of Sheila's main ambitions at this time was to play Hedvig in *The Wild Duck*, and she had hoped that she might get cast in the part. But for some reason it went to a student at the Edinburgh College who had neither the experience nor the insight to invest Hedvig with the feeling she needs and Sheila was very disappointed, but I suppose these sorts of milestone constantly approach you in our business. Some of them you can stop at and rest against and enjoy, with others life pushes you straight past, not allowing you to stop. Maybe the powers that be were beginning to feel that with a year-old son, she was no longer right to be playing fourteen-year-old girls. Gibbie was already addressing her as Old Mother Elder now. It was done in the nicest possible way and you couldn't take exception to it, especially as he referred to my mother as Young Grandmother Elder. Smarmy devil.

After that it was time for the Christmas show again. This year it was an adaptation by Robert Kemp of Neil Munro's *The Daft Days*. I think of all our Christmas shows this one was the most atmospheric to me. The scene on Hogmanay at the village cross in the snow with the bells ringing and the cast singing "A Guid New Year" was memorable. Gibbie, as producer, was determined that the song was going to be sung in the proper Scots and he borrowed the typewriter – what he called the fast-writing machine – in the office and put a paper on the notice board with details of how the words were to be pronounced. I remember his instruction for the word "mony". "Pronounced like what we all don't get enough of on Fridays."

There was a character in *The Daft Days* called Mrs McVicar. Mrs McVicar was a very small part. You might say insignificant. She came on in act two – the shop scene – bought a couple of things, had a line or two of inconsequential gossip and went out, never to be seen again. Yet Mrs McVicar was played in the course of the run by eight different actresses. A bug got into dressing room three. One by one the girls were felled by it. It was short-lived but virulent. It poleaxed you for three or four days and then people got better again, pale and shaken but able to totter on and wobble through a performance. Gradually our supply of ASMs was used up as they were thrown into various costumes and pushed on to the stage. Each ASM started her career as an understudy by playing Mrs McVicar before graduating to bigger parts. With the inevitability of Greek tragedy Pamela, Christine and Evelyn went down. There was one night we played with eight understudies, because George had also fallen by the wayside with an unrelated illness – a form of bronchitis, I think – and his part had to be taken over by Brian Carey with yet another ersatz Scots accent.

It culminated one Thursday night when the girl playing the lead, Diana Tullis, who was actually in dressing room two with Lennox and who looked as if she might avoid the scourge by being in a different room, said after the performance that she wasn't feeling very well. The symptoms sounded ominously like those we had been experiencing all too often over the last few days. This was likely to be disastrous. How could we play with four of our leading women off? Next morning we gathered for rehearsals of the next play, Roddy MacMillan's *All In Good Faith*. We hadn't actually managed to work on it very much because we'd had to rehearse so many people into rôles in *The Daft Days* and Roddy, who was playing the lead in his own play, was getting very worried about the lack of rehearsal. Diana wasn't in *All In Good Faith* so her absence was perfectly natural. But while we were partaking of the brew of the bean of Brazil word came through on Gibbie's so-called far-talking machine in the office. It was a medical report that Diana was flat out in her bed, unable to stir. We had finally run out of actresses.

"Is Sheila busy?" Lennox asked me with deceptive casualness.

I knew where that was leading. Sheila wasn't in *The Daft Days* and she was actually doing a broadcast that day, but transmission would be over by half past two. I was deputed to take a fast car – well, Pandora, actually – up to the BBC in Queen Street and ask her if she'd go on. I hurried into the Studio 2 control room and found they were just finishing the final run-through before transmission and I asked the producer if I could go through and speak to her. Permission granted, I went into the studio. Sheila saw me and I don't think I've ever seen her face change colour so quickly. We'd talked about the problems with the cast of the play and she knew we were running out of actresses so she must have had a pretty good idea what to expect before I'd said a word. Perhaps the fact that I was carrying Diana's annotated script of *The Daft Days* in my hand was something of a give-away. We had a hasty talk while the hands of the clock crept round to her transmission time. She agreed to go on that night. Well, in the circumstances what else could she say? If she'd said no we'd have had to close the theatre.

She got a taxi down to the Gateway after transmission and we ran her through the part and she went on that night with the book. Overnight and during Saturday morning she learnt the part and went on at the Saturday matinée and on Saturday night without the book at all. In my recollection she never dried once. By Monday Diana was back and the crisis was virtually over. All that frantic learning for so little!

Reckoning it up afterwards we worked it out that Lennox, Bill and I were the only people in the Company who went right through the run of *The Daft Days* playing the same part at every performance. This may have given an element of security to the proceedings but from our point of view the worst of it was walking on to the stage every night never quite sure who you were going to meet. At one point in the middle of the chaos we had got a student ASM from the

Edinburgh College to sit on the book because all the ASMs were otherwise engaged, and as Mrs McVicar VIII came on in the second act she turned to Brian Mahoney and whispered, "Who played Mrs McVicar originally?"

Gibbie got very tetchy during all this. He didn't appreciate illness. Lennox once said to me earlier in our Gateway careers:

"I don't understand Gibbie. He smokes like a chimney, he never takes any exercise, his favourite meal is pie and chips and he's never had a day's illness in his life."

This was absolutely true. He didn't know what illness was until he had a stroke while he was watching what he would call a motion picture in a cinema when he was rehearsing a television play in London at the age of 81. So he had little sympathy with illness.

But they were well named the daft days in the middle of that New Year show. However, we could claim that, like the Windmill Theatre in London, we never closed.

From *The Daft Days* we moved into the dreich days of winter. While we were doing *All In Good Faith* the company split and rehearsed two productions at the same time again and the tour went out to the Borders in February while the rest of us stayed behind. One began to get the impression that Robert was cornering the market in touring plays because this time they were taking out *The Other Dear Charmer*, though they were having to do it without me and my wig this time. We stay-at-homes did firstly a recent West End comedy, *All For Mary* which went down well. It was very quiet backstage during this one because there was only one set so no changes, and the cast consisted of Wally Carr, Marillyn, Bill, Evelyn, a nice little French actor from the French Institute called André Courtin and me. The thing I remember best about it was making the curtain speech at the end of the first Saturday matinée, because that afternoon Scotland had beaten Wales at Murrayfield, our first victory for what seemed about a century, and we'd been listening to it on my yak-box in the dressing room throughout the performance. People would exit calmly, take off from the starting blocks, sprint from the wings and clatter up the spiral staircase to dressing room five. "What's the score?" they'd ask breathlessly. Others would be glued to the yak-box with one ear and to the tannoy with the other, trying to listen to two different things at the same time, and leaving their departure for an entrance till the last possible minute. The Lord must have been watching over us as well as the Scottish team with a benevolent eye that afternoon. No one was off. I thought the audience would like to share the good news of Scotland's victory. I had visions of them slapping each other on the back with tears of relief in their eyes and shaking each other's hands. The announcement was received in a stony and puzzled silence and I realised that the average age out there was probably in the mid-seventies and few of them would even have known that the match was on that afternoon or what game I was talking about.

One more yak-box story. As I said, Gibbie disapproved of it in the dressing room. He thought it was dangerous, and he was probably right. (He was out on the tour during the Scotland–Wales international, otherwise we would probably not have dared listen to the commentary.) Nevertheless that didn't stop him from taking part in the pools syndicate I ran with little success. But one Saturday after the results had been declared and there was no dividend for Leezie Telfer hadn't won anything again and the yak-box was closed up for the week and we'd been out for tea – fish and chips at the Olympia café next door – the other next door to the Windsor – we were back making up and dressing again for the evening show and the half had been called when there was a tap at the door. Gibbie poked his head round. For some reason there was an embarrassed silence which I didn't understand. Eventually, to break it, I said.

"Hi, Gibbie."

The embarrassed silence was extended a fraction.

"Eh – the yak-box," he said at last.

"What about it?"

He emitted an embarrassed snort which was better than the embarrassed silence.

"Could I borrow it?"

I couldn't believe my ears. Here was an unexpected chance. I went into long details about how I didn't think I should lend it to him because it wasn't safe, he might be off and it would be all my fault, and I took my responsibilities in these matters very seriously . . .

I thought I did it rather well. He listened with every appearance of humility, almost of agreement.

"I'll be finished with it before the curtain goes up," he said humbly.

I started again about that not being the point, it was the principle of the thing and I'd taken a lot of stick from him over the weeks, and I worked myself into a state where I was thoroughly enjoying myself. I ended up by asking him anti-climactically what he wanted it for anyway. It appeared that he had recently recorded – the BB guess the third letter was now recording certain specific and important programmes – six of Robert McLellan's Linmill stories and the first of them went out that night between 7.15 and 7.30. I gave him the yak-box and he took it into dressing room six with him. I followed him and showed him how to raise the lid to make the thing go and I listened to the Linmill stories with him for the next six Saturdays. They were marvellous, some of the best radio I've ever heard and if they still exist, which they ought to if some blindfolded buffoon of a boffin hasn't destroyed them, they should be issued on cassette or CD as an epitaph for both Robert McLellan and Gibbie.

We followed *All For Mary* with *Black Chiffon* which was my play out, a little late in the season and it meant coming back for two weeks' rehearsal and only one week of playing in Pinero's *The Schoolmistress* and at the end of March we closed for the season.

There were a couple of significant events during the summer.

Firstly and most importantly Sheila became pregnant again. This meant that we had to alter the arrangements we'd made with John and Freddie Young to drive to London for three days to see some shows, because although Sheila came down in the car with us she felt that was enough and decided to go back in the comfort of the train. While we were in London we saw the third performance of *My Fair Lady* with Rex Harrison, Julie Andrews and Stanley Holloway which we found magical and we watched the stage at Drury Lane with its two revolves with jealous eyes. We had nothing like that at the Gateway where there were just a couple of Goblins heaving flats around.

It looked now as if Sheila's stage career was going to have to go on hold for a while, though all through the summer and the autumn she continued to broadcast, which was the ideal medium for her in the present circumstances. She could go on doing that until the last minute and people wouldn't know that this small boy they were listening to was actually great with child, though one of the producers enquired keenly about dates. "We don't want you dropping it at the microphone, darling. Not during transmission, anyway," she added thoughtfully. As she got bigger and had Simon to look after at the same time, three hours out of the house in a studio at the BBC was rather like a welcome break and it kept her in touch with what was going on.

Later in the summer I received a summons to go and have a chat with Robert Kemp. I didn't like the sound of this very much. Were they going to throw me out into the street – me with a wife and one and a half children to support? I called at the appointed time at Robert's house in Warriston Crescent and was offered some rather sticky sherry which I didn't really want and certainly didn't enjoy. Robert seemed embarrassed and my worry grew.

We talked about the weather (good), the political situation (middling), the state of the economy (bad) and other trivial things and the conversation seemed to become more and more stilted. This was most unusual. Robert was normally the easiest person to talk to. Finally he took a deep breath.

"You know we're doing *Weir of Hermiston* for the Festival this year?"

I nodded. I'd heard rumours to that effect but this was the first confirmation.

"We don't want you to play Archie," he blurted out at last.

I felt an overwhelming relief. Was that all? I'd never felt comfortable in the part and I must say it had been passing through my mind that if the rumour about *Weir* being the Festival play was true it wasn't going to do me any good appearing in either the part or the wig. In my wilder moments I'd toyed with the idea of spurning it contemptuously when and if I was asked to do it. But here the responsibility for doing so was taken out of my hands.

"Thank God," I said.

He stared at me in surprise.

"You didn't like the part?" he asked.

"The part's all right," I said, "but I don't think it liked me."

He smiled in relief that I had made what must have been the prospect of an uncomfortable interview so easy.

"We'd love to have you as a Black Brother," he said.

I thought about that for a moment and almost immediately shook my head.

"I'd rather not be in it at all," I said. "I think it would be better for everyone all round."

I'd had quite a bit of experience of people repeating a part in a different production of a play. *The Dashing White Sergeant* at Pitlochry, for instance, where I played the same part I'd played at the Gateway. I was playing opposite a girl who had also played her part at a rep in England, and we spent most of the rehearsal time saying, "When *we* did it we did it *this* way." Sometimes we almost came to blows, two people who were supposed in the context of the play to be madly in love, and we caused despair to the current producer who was trying to mount something new but didn't have our advantage: he'd never done the play before. I didn't want to cause anything like that here. The parallel wasn't exact because I wouldn't be playing the same part, but I could foresee that being in the same play again might cause similar problems. Besides, the Black Brothers were all black-haired as their name implied and that would mean a wig, not the same wig as the Archie wig, but possibly worse.

Robert agreed and poured me out another sherry, finishing the bottle, so fortunately there couldn't be any more. I took a deep breath. It seemed to be an afternoon for deep-breathing exercises.

"You do want me after that, though?" I asked.

"Of course."

That was a relief too. It was probably the earliest I'd ever known about the situation for the forthcoming season.

"Who's going to play Archie?" I asked.

"Frank Wylie."

"Great casting," I said.

Frank was small and intense, exactly what Archie should be, and I could see him playing off Tom as Lord Weir with a lot of sparks.

We parted on Robert's doorstep with mutual expressions of high esteem and I went home a great deal happier than I'd arrived.

I saw Frank playing Archie and he was infinitely better than I was. And he had a wig that looked natural too. There is no justice.

We then went into the play which Gibbie had gone to London to do and which I had failed to get into, *Keep In A Cool Place*. This production was remarkable for Pamela, who played one of the daughters-in-law who was a dancer. On her own initiative and without any prompting she put herself through an intensive course of training and by the time we got to the first night she was doing high kicks and splits with the best of them and we were all really very impressed. After that we did what I believe was the first production outside London of John Osborne's *Look Back In Anger*. This was very daring at the time, particularly considering where most of our audience came from, and during the performances there were odd grumblings about it and occasionally a thump of a seat being vacated indignantly as its owner left the theatre in anger – without looking back. We followed that with Alexander Reid's *The Warld's Wonder* which I'd been in the première of at the Citizens' five years before. Alex had written a new scene to open the first act and had greatly improved it.

For some years there had been an idea floating around for a Scottish Repertory interchange. This must have been a fiendishly difficult thing to organise but finally it became a practical proposition this year. Perth, Dundee, Citizens' and the Gateway all agreed to mount one play to take to each other's theatres, which meant that each company's play would run for a total of four weeks. We revived *The Penny Wedding* and we opened it at the Gateway before taking it out on the interchange. There was a bit of excitement during the Gateway run. We had already heard that Tyrone Guthrie was going to direct *The Thrie Estaits* at the Festival again the following year, and now we were told that he was coming to see our production with a view to casting. Sure enough, he arrived one night, sat through the performance and then asked to meet us all on the stage afterwards.

There was a section in the third act of *The Penny Wedding*, when George, playing a retired master baker, looked back at his attempt to win the gold medal for macaroons at the Paris Exhibition many years before. It was a deliciously funny and rather gentle scene and George played it beautifully. One memorable line concerned the moment when the judges were making their decision. "The silence was such that you could have heard a scone rise," said George.

We were sitting round the stage as Gibbie brought the great man on from the wings, looking exactly as I remembered him from dressing room five. He was charming and direct, said there would be no Gateway Festival production next year as almost everyone would be employed in mounting *The Thrie Estaits* at the Assembly Hall, that there would be parts for all of us, we could rely on that and not to book holidays any time before or during the Festival. He made one or two polite remarks and prepared to leave again. As he passed George he clapped him on the shoulder.

"Most moving about the macaroons," he said.

The following week we took *The Penny Wedding* to the Citizens', the first time I'd worked there since the Peter Potter season, and we did a week of fantastic business. We moved on to Dundee where I was able to stay with an aunt and uncle, and one night my family almost booked the old rep in Nicoll Street solid. I had two uncles, three aunts, my father and my sister out front. There may have been several cousins as well, but possibly there wasn't room for them all. Then the next week we moved on to Perth. We did good business everywhere. Which is more than could be said for the other companies. Of course we never saw any of the other productions, as they never saw ours. Citizens' did *The Cherry Orchard*, Dundee did Sartre's *Crime Passionel*, and Perth did Shaw's *Caesar and Cleopatra*. Reading a list of the plays done at that very important but never to be repeated interchange, you have to wonder what the basic aim of it was. We were obviously going for the commercial, get as many bums on seats as possible, while the others seemed to be concentrating on the artistic challenge and therefore the kudos. Maybe all four of us should have moved towards the middle ground, partly to justify the Arts Council supporting the experiment but also to encourage them to believe that all the companies were capable of raking in a certain amount of money to justify the expense and therefore perhaps make it an annual event. We spent a lot of our days on tour rehearsing our next play which was *Boyd's Shop* by St John Ervine and once we'd brought that back and dress rehearsed it and opened it on the Monday night before our usual audience, we moved on to our second Ibsen, *A Doll's House*, and on the Sunday before it opened our second child was born. I got the call from the gynaecologist at about half past ten in the morning. He said, "You've got another son. I haven't got his weight yet but he's a whopper." He was. He weighed in at 9lb 13½oz which was all very fine, but although as the phrase goes mother and son were both doing well, he lost a lot of that initial weight after birth so you wonder why he bothered to put so much of it on before. We called him David, which was a family name on both sides. He stood out for size when he was exhibited to me through the fish-tank window of the crèche that afternoon. He was as bald as a coot and seemed to remain that way for a long time, but actually his hair was coming through surreptitiously and absolutely ash-blonde which made it difficult to see. Before I left them that first afternoon Sheila gave me a little Matchbox double-decker toy bus and said, "Give that to Simon. Tell him it's from David and he brought it with him specially." She has always been wise in the ways of the world. I followed instructions, Simon received it with wonder and gratitude and I like to think it was at least partly that gesture which made the pair of them such good friends through all these later years. When I brought Sheila and David home a week or so later Simon was standing on the gate eagerly awaiting his brother's arrival, though his face fell when he saw how small the new addition was. He may have weighed in at 9lb 13½oz but this was not yet someone you could play football with.

I played a very unshaven Dr Rank in *A Doll's House*. This was because the forthcoming New Year show was to be a revival of *The Forrigan Reel* and I was playing Grant of Forrigan this time round. Lennox suggested I grew my beard for the part, so I started straightaway. I hated the first week or so when the stubble was itchy and stuck to the pillow-case and it simply looked as if I'd forgotten to shave but after that I grew quite keen on it. I'd never grown my beard before and it came through healthy and gingery and was altogether quite impressive which satisfied my curiosity as to what it would turn out like. And it saved me from sticking one of the damned things on every night and twice on matinée days though Sheila used to look at it with extreme distaste and mutter "Yuch!" with increasing force.

Between *A Doll's House* and *The Forrigan Reel* we spent Christmas week doing a kind of nativity play by Tom called *Miracle at Midnight*. This was a moving, poetic piece which contained five assorted character types, a shepherd, a snowman, a displaced person, the earth mother, a business man, all used very skilfully as facets of the Christmas story. The action was interspersed with carols. Guess who got to sing the carols? That's right. Those of us who weren't playing the five main characters. We looked forward to this with some trepidation, none of us being particularly brilliant singers. But there was a miracle, not at midnight, but during the day when Iain Robertson who had been a close friend of the Company since he had actually appeared in *Marigold* and who had designed all our excellent programme covers in their familiar yellow borders, came in to teach us to sing. He knew he wasn't dealing with singers. It didn't bother him. As far as *Miracle At Midnight* was concerned we were just a group of itinerant carol singers and what we lacked in technique we made up for in sincerity. We began to feel a stirring of interest. This wasn't just sing and be damned. There was a challenge here. A big one, because these carols were unaccompanied and Iain issued most of them in four parts and used a tuning fork to get us going in the right key. I don't think any of us had sung in four parts before. Few of us had sung in one part other than in the bath. We tried them out. The result, after some experiment, became bearable. It got better as we rehearsed and as enthusiasm grew. Iain was an inspiring teacher. "Steam in boilers, cheeks in brassières, go!" he'd say and we'd be smiling when we started and kept smiling till we finished, filled with a strange kind of contentment and satisfaction which I don't think any of us fully understood but which we all appreciated finding among us.

The carol singing that year, and the following year when *Miracle at Midnight* was repeated for a week's run, was one of the highlights of our time at the Gateway. The carols started as an integral part of the play when we wandered on to the stage between scenes in scarves and winter pullovers, but by the time we opened we were singing more of them after the performance was over and inviting the audience to join in with us, which they did with remarkable enthusiasm and they left us reluctantly in the end to return home. I don't think the sound we raised between us was particularly beautiful, falling fractionally below King's College Cambridge standard, but the feeling was tremendous.

What gave this perfectly ordinary singing of perfectly ordinary carols in perfectly ordinary voices this extraordinary feeling? I think it was because it epitomised all our work at the Gateway. It was the family getting together which always seemed to be the case anyway, but getting together at Christmas gave it a special significance. Everyone sang the carols as equals. Actors, actresses, stage managers, ASMs, even Alice Marshall came down from the wardrobe and took part. It was a presentation of what we were all about. No wonder it was memorable.

This later *Forrigan Reel* had Gibbie and John Macrae playing their original parts of the MacAlpines while Lennox wound herself up and became a clock again. We had the longest run of any New Year show. *The Forrigan Reel* lasted for six weeks and was virtually my last show of the season.

When it was over I shaved off my now very impressive beard and returned to normal, thereby pleasing Sheila no end and terrifying the daylights out of Simon. The growth had been so slow that he hadn't noticed but suddenly there appeared this bare-faced stranger who seemed to be very friendly with his mother and it took him a while to get used to the normal me again. David never noticed a thing. At three months regular meals were more important than personal appearance.

I'd been having a quiet rethink about life since David was born. There were now four of us and although my salary at the Gateway had gone up to twelve pounds a week it was becoming a bit of a strain trying to keep a family on it. I had been relying more frequently on the schools broadcasts and therefore more and more often I'd found myself asking off rehearsals to go and do one of these three hour epics. It wasn't just me. Bill and Christine were being offered a great deal of radio now too. This was unfair on the Company, though Lennox said that she understood that nowadays people couldn't live comfortably on what the Company could afford to pay, and a certain amount of co-operation was inevitable. This was a generous attitude, but it didn't strike me as being terribly satisfactory from anyone's point of view, so with some reluctance I dropped out for the rest of the season, missing the last three plays.

As it happens it didn't quite work out as a complete break, because the Company had decided to try to mount a short summer season of successful comedies from the past year or two for a week at a time. They would start with the old stand-by *The Heart Is Highland*, which only involved Lennox, then there would be a week of Moray McLaren's *Muckle Ado*, followed by A B Paterson's *The Open* and winding up with William Templeton's *Keep In A Cool Place*, so we reassembled to re-rehearse the last three plays for a fortnight. This, the Council felt, if successful, would do away with much of the huge gap in the middle of the summer when there was no work with the Company and which often lost us good actors and actresses to other ventures.

It was a great idea in theory. In practice it was a disaster. It was a hot summer, so people weren't prepared to come out and spend the long light evenings in a dark, stuffy auditorium. Most of our audience had already seen these plays anyway and summer visitors to Edinburgh simply weren't interested in a theatre tucked away down Leith Walk. We played to rows of empty seats each night and it was depressing hearing your voice echo round a virtually empty theatre, especially when you compared it with the reception we'd had at the original runs.

It certainly shortened the summer recess to some extent, though it was quite obvious that, having had their fingers severely burnt the Company wouldn't repeat the exercise, and there were still about eight weeks between the end of the summer season and the start of rehearsals for *The Thrie Estaits*.

The Thrie Estaits is a puzzle. In its original form it's an eight-hour dramatised sermon written by Sir David Lindsay of the Mount for the young King James V advising him on the responsibilities of kingship and government. Its relevance to today is a bit misty. The art in preparing it for a modern audience starts with the cutting down of the original text to a manageable size. This Robert did superbly well. He was also well served by his original cast in 1948 who breathed life into the stereotypical characters. But the main advantage for that production and the later ones up till and including 1959 was in its producer. Tony Guthrie took a fairly verbose script and wrung glory out of it. Movement, pageantry, crashing music with dozens of trumpets, banners, mass entrances and exits through the audience, anything to delight the eye and stop people trying to make sense of the dialogue. 1959 was the last time Guthrie produced it. I think by then he'd had enough and he felt he was churning out productions without anything new to say. The play has been revived since, of course, but each revival has been inevitably a shadow of Guthrie's production and sometimes a pale replica of Robert's script.

I'd never done it before and it was very exciting to be concerned in this production. I played Temporalitie, one of the three estates who sits on the stage throughout the first half, listens to the debate and says nothing and does exactly the same through most of the second half and says little more. And sitting there in the stuffy Assembly Hall in those thick costumes was hellishly uncomfortable, especially on matinée days. The place wasn't designed to circulate air properly and your costume didn't have a chance to dry out before the second show and you longed for someone to walk past you fast on the stage and create a draught. But to watch Guthrie put this monumental production together, although he'd done it before and the experimental phase was well past, was a privilege and a pleasure. He strode non-stop around the stage in the Assembly Hall, up and down the steps, covering miles each day, imperiously snapping his fingers, eyes restlessly moving, missing nothing, a dynamo running overtime, throwing instructions in all directions, apparently disconnected but always pertinent. In their way the Guthrie phrases were as memorable as the Gibbie ones. To Wally Carr when he appeared in a black wig as one of the Vices: "Can't wear that, you look like Tanya Moiseiwich's mother-in-law." To an actor having trouble how to interpret his part: "Go home, study it tonight, come back and astonish us in the morning." But his more specific instructions on how to play a part were succinct and immediately understandable. To Lennox and Jean Taylor Smith, playing the Verities: " *You* are Miss Women's Institute. And *you* are Miss Salvation Army." To Pamela, playing the Prioress who is dramatically revealed late in the play as a scarlet woman: "Think babies." In each case two or three words went right to the heart of the matter and were better and more instructive than the longest and most convoluted psychological discussion. And the endless patience as elements refused to come together but finally did, and the dress rehearsal which, possibly through his own exhaustion and certainly that of the cast, he brought to a premature close at two o'clock in the morning with the last quarter of an hour of the play, including the hanging of the Vices, still not done.

This was something big, bigger than we'd ever done at the Gateway, bigger than we were ever likely to do there and we thrilled and marvelled and returned after the opening to start rehearsing for our first couthy Scots comedy of the season *The Honours of Drumlie* by James Scotland feeling slightly deprived of excitement and purpose. This was unfair on *The Honours* which was a very funny play about redcoats seeking the civic plate in a Jacobite town and supposed dead bodies lying on tables and running around in winding sheets and much dilly-dallying with serving wenches.

Things were quieter at the Gateway than they had been during the weeks of the Festicle and the rough and tumble of hundreds of folk milling round the Assembly Hall. Visitors stood out a great deal more in Elm Row. There had always been visitors of course, particularly in dressing room three – the girls' room. Holmes Carlile had been a regular and had now gone so far as to carry Christine off – before *The Thrie Estaits*, if you please – and marry her and live happily ever after. Evelyn was either fancy free or playing her cards very close to her chest and there didn't seem to be anyone permanent there at this time. It was later that she emigrated to Ayr, married a doctor and became firstly Mrs Douglas Russell and subsequently the mother of two sons and a daughter.

It was funny how news and rumour filtered upstairs to the men's dressing rooms which sometimes became almost as excited as number three. But there was a new figure who began to appear occasionally. Bill Simpson had left the Company to go to Scottish Television and in his place an outsider appeared and began to stalk Pamela. He was short and stocky and was in the Royal Navy and his name was Desmond Kelly.

We – the men – always felt suspicious about swains who hung around our girls. It was almost as if we had a proprietorial interest in their welfare and felt that all followers should have an interview with us to judge their suitability. But we were really very broad-minded about these suitors and accepted them as a necessary evil of life. We obviously weren't very observant, though, because what none of us realised was that Desmond had actually been around for a long time, long before Bill. I think we can excuse ourselves because Bill had been very much to the forefront for some time.

In any case I don't think anyone liked Desmond very much, and this was probably because he made no attempt to like any of us. He found it difficult to conceal his disdain for people in the theatrical business and it was quite clear that one of his main reasons for declaring an interest in Pamela was to ensure her departure from the unconventional world of entertainment. We found this hard to stomach. Unlike most other professions at that time an actress's position was, as it is now, absolutely equal to that of an actor. Her place is in the business, not being exclusively domestic in the home and this equality of the sexes was jealously guarded. In most other professions equal opportunity is a comparatively recent phenomenon. Pamela had as much right as any of us to her career and to sympathy and encouragement from a future husband with any generosity of spirit. To abandon it would be a waste of all her training and, more importantly, her talent. We said many nasty and possibly untrue things about Desmond. Gibbie referred to him as "the fat sailor from Portsmouth."

Meanwhile we were working our way through the autumn season. *French Without Tears*, which I wasn't in, then a new play by Ronald Mavor called *The Keys of Paradise* which concerned an anaesthetist who was hooked on his own anaesthetics, a common enough topic in today's world but a ground-breaking and startling theme then. We'd got Richard Mathews from the former Wilson Barrett Company to play the lead and the rest of us hung around in white coats and stethoscopes and discussed medical ethics and listened to him talk.

Then Sheila succumbed to temptation. She had settled contentedly into a time of busy domesticity, punctuated with quite a few broadcasts when she could leave her mother in charge of the two grandsons, something granny was perfectly happy to do. But then she was offered the part of one of the old ladies in *Arsenic And Old Lace* at the Gateway. Well. This was an offer she couldn't refuse and domestic arrangements were altered so that she could do it. Granny was perfectly willing though slightly hesitant because David was not the placid child his brother was. He was, in fact, a holy terror, and for years Sheila said if he'd come first there wouldn't have been a second. Never still, into everything. Cheerful, laughing, utterly likeable. He's never changed. Just got louder. But we worked out how to manage it and Sheila enjoyed herself thoroughly. She and Lennox made a wonderful pair of old biddies, poisoning elderly men to save them from their loneliness. Pamela played her last part with us as the love interest, Elaine, and we had a tremendous run.

I don't know how the Company got asked to Pamela's wedding. Maybe she had been stronger-minded than she had seemed. John Young and I had a broadcast on the day so we were only able to dash into a taxi and get to the reception just as it was breaking up and the bride and groom were preparing to leave. Sheila and Freddie, John's wife, had been together at the service and the reception because of our absence and they met us at the door as we arrived to see Pamela, still looking absolutely stunning in her bridal dress, with the fat sailor from Portsmouth in full naval uniform by her side, before they went to change to go away.

"See that sword?" said Freddie. "I'll bet he has it in bed with him tonight."

And so they rode off into the sunset. Today Pamela has two stalwart sons and two lovely daughters, all of whom take after their mother, and a growing collection of grandchildren and no husband because he's gone off with another woman. It's very easy to sit here at this distance of time and say I told you so. But the story has a happy ending. Pamela is back in the business, not under her original name of Pamela Bain, because when she reapplied for entry to Equity they said they had someone of the name of Pamela Bain already on their list so she would have to change it. This is quite obviously a mistake on Equity's part and they never erased her name from the list when she got an Honorary Withdrawal at the time of her marriage. Nowadays she's Pamela Kelly, which is a pity. No one calls her Pea-Brain any more.

After *Arsenic and Old Lace* came *The Master of Ballantrae* in which I played Henry Durie, the good brother with David MacMillan as the wicked one. The main feature of the play was the sword fight between the two brothers and we spent more time rehearsing that than we did the play and we never got it right. How one of us didn't decapitate the other or at least lose a few fingers I shall never know. We certainly sustained cuts and scratches.

Lennox had asked me early in the season if I'd like to try a little adapting and I'd expressed interest. The Company were wanting to do *The Ghost Train*, I can't think why, but they felt that, maybe with memories of *Rope* still reasonably fresh in mind, it might not be a good idea to set it in its original period of the 20s and if they were going to bring it up to date why not go the whole hog and transfer it from its Cornish setting to a Scottish one? I remembered my vow never to write another play for the stage after *Outrageous Briefs*, but I thought this wouldn't exactly be breaking it. It would just be bending it a little. So I convinced myself and took it on. It was mainly the first act which required alteration, changing the minor branch railway line in Cornwall to a tiny wayside station somewhere on the Inverness-Kyle of Lochalsh line. This I did. I was particularly proud of one piece of rewritten dialogue. In the original play one of the characters asks the stationmaster where the nearest town is. The stationmaster says "Truro." "Strewth!" says the Inquisitor. "No, sir. Truro," says the stationmaster. Transferring the scene to the West Highlands I'd hit on a brilliant substitute. "Where's the nearest town?" "Kyle." "Hell!" "No, sir. Kyle." On the first night the Inquisitor said to Gibbie, playing the stationmaster, "Where's the nearest town?" "Kyle," said Gibbie. "Damn!" said the Inquisitor. "No, sir. Kyle," said Gibbie philosophically. Not unnaturally the gag fell flat. I was very angry.

The Ghost Train didn't really work. I don't think it does nowadays. We replaced gun-running in Cornwall in the original with rocket range sabotage in the Outer Isles by Russian spies but it didn't breathe life and verisimilitude into the piece.

After *The Late Christopher Bean*, which I wasn't in, we revived *Miracle At Midnight* and all our carol singing from the previous year and then mounted a stirring rendition of *Rob Roy*, adapted by Robert with music by Iain Robertson. It was pantomime stuff and quite acceptable and it did well at the box office. I had the showy double of the two Osbaldistone brothers which was great fun. At one point, playing the fox-hunting brother, I had to dash on to the stage with a drawn sword – something we were all doing most of the time anyway – sing a number with my three stage sons, rather like a barber shop quartette, then go off again. One night I dashed on and the hilt of the sword got caught in a curtain at the entrance. I tugged it free. It came away quite easily and I was aware of it bumping against my leg on the rebound. But as we went into the number I began to hear whispers starting in the audience and that unmistakable restlessness which means that something is going wrong somewhere. It was one of those terribly worrying occasions when your first thought is that your flies are undone and everyone knows it except you. But I didn't have flies on the breeches I was wearing. They buttoned up the side. A little later as I took a step on the stage I felt squelching in my shoe. Carolling away, I looked down and the white stocking on my right leg was almost totally red.

This was a disconcerting sight to meet in the middle of a number but I managed to finish it with my usual *sangfroid*, though slightly *tremolo*, strode off the stage and found myself being enveloped by two or three ASMs armed with the Company first-aid box, plasters and bandages, a bottle of Dettol and a clean pair of white stockings. The only thing missing was a bottle of smelling salts. They had all seen what had happened much more clearly than I had. The sword point, in being dragged clear of the curtain, had stabbed me in the side of the leg. My shoe was wet with blood. The stocking was wringing with it. I peeled it off there in the wings, got the wound dabbed with Dettol and had a plaster applied to it. The wound was quite small but the plaster was big in case the blood continued to seep out. All this attention was really quite fun but there wasn't time to revel in it. I had to pull on the clean white stocking, attach it to the size thirty-six suspender belt and I was just ready in time for my next entrance. One of our ASMs, Liz Wood – she who had played Mrs McVicar originally in *The Daft Days* – was actually a qualified doctor and she whispered that she wasn't sure if I should go on again, I'd lost quite a bit of blood, so I said there didn't seem to be any alternative and if she wanted to go on thinking about it to let me know her conclusion when we got to the interval, and then I was back on. The plaster patch was very obvious under the thin white stocking and was decidedly anachronistic, but at least it seemed to have stopped the flow of blood. The extraordinary thing is I never felt a thing until they dabbed it with Dettol. No pain, either with the point of the sword going in or afterwards. But I've still got the scar and I show it to my grandchildren as if it were a war wound and bore the pants off them. I suppose I was lucky not to get blood-poisoning because the sword wasn't exactly pure clean steel.

Rob Roy ran for four weeks, the shortest of any Gateway Company New Year show. It was also the last production of the season in the theatre. True, the touring company went out on their annual invasion of the Borders but as far as the theatre itself was concerned that was that. The Company had never closed so early before and the reason was financial. Bums were deserting seats for television, there was rampant inflation everywhere, the Arts Council grant didn't keep pace with it and the previous disastrous summer had drained reserves from the coffers.

There was a wind of change blowing through the place anyway. Quite a cold wind, it seemed to us. There were changes in the Gateway Company Council and there was concern over what to do to counteract the insidious advance of the goggle-box. All right, the television picture was black and white and still very hazy and broke down a lot, but it moved and the small screen showed you views the theatre couldn't attempt. You could shift rapidly from location to location to maintain the interest and the movement. How did you provide people with comparable shows they wanted to see when you were desperately short of money? How did you drag people out of their cosy sitting rooms in the first place to face a cold journey to a theatre and an even colder journey home afterwards?

These were questions which would have to be tackled and they were tackled with greater and lesser success, but that was after my time and I had no personal experience of the developing struggle which all theatres were experiencing. I did one more play early in the following season. This was *Master John Knox* written by Robert Kemp for the Church of Scotland Home Board to celebrate the Church's four hundredth anniversary. In it Tom played John Knox and Gibbie, Norman and I played a trio of soldiers who acted as a kind of chorus to the action. We were the only remaining members of the old Company and by the time I did it I had already severed my connection with much regret and many nostalgic backward glances. It had been a long, hard seven years, but I wouldn't have missed them for anything.

Epilogue

For the last few weeks I've been wallowing in nostalgia and memories. I'm not sure that this is a particularly healthy situation to get oneself into, but I've got to admit I've enjoyed it in a macabre sort of way. I've remembered things I thought I'd forgotten, many of which should have remained forgotten. And I'm sure there are many other things I simply haven't remembered at all. A psychological block, probably. I speculated earlier on about the problems of rose-coloured spectacles and I think by now I've learnt that rose for nostalgia can very quickly turn to red for danger.

One of the questions that's been slopping around in the back of my mind is – could The Edinburgh Gateway Company be revived? If some benevolent magician were to wave a wand and cry, "Here's your theatre back just as it was and here you are just as you were. Abracadabra, start again," could it be done?

Well, let's face it, the answer is a pretty definite no.

The Edinburgh Gateway Company was of its time. Relevant, vital, inventive, stimulating. But the idea that it could be revived, with all of us miraculously young again, fresh and enthusiastic, occupying the building as it was and starting a re-run of those twelve years, doesn't actually bear thinking about, especially if you're talking about trying to do it in today's environment. In any case things are never so good the second time round.

Television has inevitably taken its toll on the type of theatre we usually presented. The plays are dated and many of them scarcely worth reviving. Not all, but most. And those that might be revivable would only be so for their historical interest. The staging would be seen as clumsy and tedious to audiences fed on the speed of change and the naturalism and incredible variety of every set-up on television. The theatre we knew and loved couldn't bear comparison with that, and if it tried the audiences wouldn't come to see us and if they did they'd be bored to distraction. Theatre audiences are smaller now and more sophisticated. They demand more, they see more and they're a great deal more discriminating. They've changed just as styles of plays and presentations have changed. What modern theatre has seats facing only in one direction? What modern theatre uses a proscenium arch and a curtain? Although these things are still viable they are tending to become archaic. We may regret this but it's a fact. The theatre has been forced to try to present plays with the speed and directness that television can achieve. This means in practice fewer cumbersome sets which take ages to change. It means more simple backgrounds to play against, backgrounds which can suggest rather than present, and the subtleties of theatrical lighting are many and varied nowadays with so many technical improvements, far more so than they were in our Gateway days.

It's what's called progress. It's inevitable and it's not something to weep salt tears over. The old order changeth, giving place to new. 'Twas ever thus. I could go on with the clichés.

So no. We couldn't achieve a miraculous renewal of youth and come back and do the whole *sordid* thing again, only better, as Gibbie might have said. And if we have any sense we won't try – or encourage anyone else to try.

This doesn't invalidate what we did. Those of us who are still shuffling around are proud of it. Why shouldn't we be? And I like the feeling that today's young actors and actresses – sorry. Actors only. They're all the same now, aren't they, though I'm ashamed to say I can still spot the difference – have a respect for what we did. But that respect seems to be mixed with a slight air of indulgence, almost of disbelief. I don't think they want to do the same sort of thing in the same sort of way, but I think that they can see with that invaluable commodity hindsight that there is a pretty sturdy bridge between what we did and what they are doing and that something like The Edinburgh Gateway Company was a very important stepping stone in a very long journey the end of which is not yet anywhere in sight. And let's hope the end never appears, because if it does they and we will all be in the doldrums.

And I like to think that the old Gateway is still there, different in outlook and purpose, but still lively, still vital, still encouraging the art of acting and theatre as we did.

It's fifty years since The Edinburgh Gateway Company was founded and so it's only natural that in that time we've lost a good many friends and colleagues. It would be tedious to recall them all here, but I'd like to append the names of those who were closest to me and/or who influenced me most and who I never had a chance to thank or say goodbye to at the time. Some died too young, some died at a normal age and some died very old. It's a purely personal list and it satisfies me as much as such a list can satisfy anyone.

Sadie Aitken; Nell Ballantyne; Brian Carey; Walter Carr; George Davies; James Gibson; Robert Kemp; Roddy MacMillan; Duncan Macrae; Lennox Milne; Peter Potter; Iain Robertson; Bill Simpson; Frank Wylie; John Young.